VOCĀTIŌ

IMAGING A VISIBLE CHURCH

C. ANDREW DOYLE

Foreword by Peter Block

CHURCH
PUBLISHING
INCORPORATED

Unless otherwise noted, the Scripture quotations contained herein are from the New Revised Standard Version Bible, copyright © 1989 by the Division of Christian Education of the National Council of Churches of Christ in the U.S.A. Used by permission. All rights reserved.

Church Publishing
19 East 34th Street
New York, NY 10016
www.churchpublishing.org

Cover design by Paul Soupiset
Typeset by PerfecType, Nashville, Tennessee

Library of Congress Cataloging-in-Publication Data

A record of this book is available from the Library of Congress.

ISBN-13: 978-1-64065-117-3 (pbk.)
ISBN-13: 978-1-64065-118-0 (ebook)

Printed in the United States of America

VOCĀTIŌ

Woe to you religious leaders, hypocrites! For you cross the sea and land to make a single convert, and you make the new convert twice as much a child of hell as yourselves. (Matt. 23:15)

Contents

Foreword: A Neighborly Narrative

By Peter Block

This book is a prophetic invitation to reimagine the functioning of the Church. It calls us, first, to follow a more authentic and communal way of being a Church together and, second, to activate the Church into healing the woundedness of our culture by restoring our neighborliness in community. My intention is to speak to why this book is important to us all and how we might respond to its invitation, whether from Church or not Church, faith or not faith.

There are two ideas that create a context for this book: The first is to be specific about how our ingestion of the beliefs and values of the free market consumer economy has both rearranged the landscape of our soul and created institutional cultures that prevent us from living out our deeper purpose. The second is to talk about how these beliefs produce a sense of isolation and incompetence that lead us to lose faith in the power of neighbors and community. The impact and cost of this doubt is that we have surrendered our collective capacity to take into our own hands our well-being, our livelihood, health, safety, and the care for our children and those whose lives are most vulnerable.

The invitation of Bishop Doyle addresses both of these issues: the transformation of the contemporary Church and the mission-driven possibility of reestablishing a neighborly economy based on the abundance inherent in our faith. This contests the scarcity mentality that now dominates our narrative, our ideologies, and our way of being with each other.

The Imperial Economy

We live in culture that is increasingly determined not by the laws of nations, or the covenants of God, but by the laws of business and its affection for management solutions to human problems. It tries to treat the human condition through ideological beliefs that are most visible in a free market consumer economy. The liturgy of that ideology is the incessant and well-financed glorification of efficiency, speed, commodification, and scale.

These beliefs originated in and grew through the long development of industrialization, and at this point they have spread into every corner of the culture, the community, and our institutional life. This ideology governs how we live, even to the question of who cooks our dinner. It has side effects that impact our souls, namely the way we choose to isolate ourselves and compete with each other. This influence is so ingrained that we rarely see it as a problem, and when we do, we look to the Imperial Economy to solve it for us. We have been sold the idea that flat screens cure our loneliness, crowd funding makes us more cooperative, and shipping our children to Africa for two educational weeks contributes to world peace.

The Tenets of the Imperial Economy

Efficiency means that the more we can produce at the lowest cost, the more value we can deliver, the more sales and profit we can expect. This is called comparative advantage. The cost most amenable to reduction is labor cost. Wage cost. Benefit cost. Cost cutting calls for outsourcing our labor cost to contractors that can seemingly operate more efficiently by not paying market rate for people, not paying for health benefits, or such luxuries as holidays and family leave.

Better yet, our attraction to efficiency leads us to automate every transaction we can get our hands on. It was machines in the beginning. Now we see the magical emergence of BOTS and artificial intelligence. Siri and Alexa are household names; they live rent free in our homes and are our watchful companions.

The business culture has also developed a love of *speed*. Speed is God; time is the devil. We have come to believe that we are running out of time. There is too little time. Time is a consumable that must be well used. We eat fast food. We have no time to cook, or even to pick up a prepared meal. The world must be delivered to our doorstep.

For efficiency and speed to reign, we are required to *commodify* what we exchange and who and what we care about. People are interchangeable and in many cases obstacles to performance. In the tech world, people are considered "friction," something that slows down a transaction. In a commodified world, consistency, control, and predictability are values in and of themselves. The primary task of management, whether in government, a business, or a church, is to take surprise out of the future.

The Imperial Economy has an insatiable need for *scale*. Size matters. Any innovation in the free market consumer world must face the question, "Can you take it to scale?" This is the essential measure of things. If you cannot take it to scale, why would we invest in what you have created? Globalization is just one expression of this: the domestic market is too small, we must seek the low-hanging fruit in countries where labor cost is low and the absence of regulations makes for a more favorable climate for private enterprise. We see the love of scale all around us. Universities have to offer online courses; people purchase followers on Twitter to bolster their brand. Even in the compassion industries, if you want funding, you have to prove you can replicate in many places what you do here. It is called leveraging our investment dollars, even when the dollars are an expression of love.

Parallel to these beliefs is the love of individualism and competition. Its simplest expression is when children enter first grade and are placed in individual competition with their peers. In that moment, which we accept without question, we convert children from learners to performers, and in that act, as educator Ward Mailliard points out, we steal a piece of their humanity.

These covenants of commerce have worked well for businesses and brands. They produced upward mobility, created a strong middle class and fed the belief that the future will be a highway of continuous progress. These beliefs have been so compelling that they have captured our consciousness, our way of being together, and our collective value systems. Now this imperial model of private enterprise dictates how all of our institutions function and how we function within them.

Some Examples

A key function of *government* once was to care for the common good and to be a caretaker for democratic values. Now it is asked to run like a business: efficiency, speed, commodification, and scale. If government cannot deliver on these business criteria, the function is outsourced. We have privatized the prisons, the highways, the parking meters, public safety, and the military.

The Imperial Economy has also invaded *education*. Instead of developing the whole child as a citizen and thinking of education as a keystone of democracy, we now believe that education's primary purpose is to develop good employees to feed the productivity of the marketplace. School now is a place to prepare our children to get a job. There is a standardized core curriculum, standardized testing, a computer in the hands of every child, and a race to the top. We give priority to a curriculum of science, engineering, and technology with the claim that they are needed to maintain market and competitive dominance in the world. Where did the arts and humanities go?

We see the same effects in health care, not-for-profit management, and, to the point of this book, the faith community and the Church. We find a small example in how religious and educational institutions view their endowments. Most trustees of endowments believe their job is to protect that money and grow it, rather than to aggressively invest it in the good cause for which it was given. There are towers of capital in our cities that could drastically reduce suffering or provide education for all if the endowment money were spent. But if I think my job is to hold and grow the money, I distribute my 5 percent and protect the rest. Under the pressure of empire, all of our institutions struggle to fulfill their original purpose and create environments fit for human habitation. Thus, this book offers a much needed call for reimagining the Church.

Effects on Community

When you look through the lens of the Imperial Economy, you see how market and management values are defining our lives. By embracing the imperial value system, our neighbors and neighborhoods have become incapacitated. We have come to believe that we can outsource the raising of our children to the schools. We expect the police to keep us safe, and pharmaceutical companies to keep us healthy. This leaves us dependent on institutions to look after what we traditionally were competent to care for ourselves.

What is not widely recognized is that where there is strong social capital—a term for neighbors who trust each other and work together to make the place better—there is strong evidence that children learn more and function as citizens more effectively. Where you have solid neighborhood connections, money is spent locally and the livelihood of all is enhanced. These places are safer because the eyes of the neighborhood are on the street. Also, all the indicators of health improve when people are less isolated and connected with others in a place. When we are active in one local association, our life span increases by half a year.

Eliminating Poverty, Drug Abuse, and Violence

The imperial economic ideology has been the dominant way of thinking not only in our institutions, but also in working on our larger societal problems. It has dominated our attempts to deal with poverty, drugs, and violence. We have fought a war on poverty, a war on drugs, and wars to end all wars. By now it should be clear that market values are useless in these pursuits. We cannot use more diagnosis or look to efficiency, scale, and speed to end poverty, reduce drug abuse, or end violence.

If we have the courage to seriously consider eliminating poverty, drug abuse, and violence, it will take a major shift in thinking and focus. One framing for this shift is to think of it as a switch from the imperial narrative to a neighborly narrative—what Bishop Doyle calls a shalom community. On these difficult fronts, the Church, with its commitment to compassion and care for the least of us, already has the language and history and text to move toward the shift. We need a different way of thinking about these issues than better management, more programs, better measurement, clearer goals, and more experts. The Church and this book offer this different way of thinking.

> If we are to deepen our understanding of the work—the vocation—of the people of God in the future Church, we must come to terms with the fact that we are called to be a community that is completely different from the world around us. (p. 10)

The neighborly narrative would have us stop believing that poverty, drugs, and violence are problems to be solved and call us to see them as symptoms of something deeper—symptoms of the isolation and scarcity mentality that are the inevitable, and not accidental, effects of an imperial ideology. Empire cannot sustain itself unless we are convinced to compete against each other. We sustain empire when we believe we are autonomous and on our own—the essence of individualism. We nourish empire when we keep looking for leaders and institutions, church and priests included, who can keep us safe.

The neighborly narrative would have us end the belief that it is in our nature and interests to always want more. Empire promises us a predictable and measurable future. It has convinced us that whatever we have is not enough. Not enough time. Not enough wealth. Not enough stuff. We have to stop believing that we must be able to purchase all that matters: health, children's well-being, safety, pharmaceuticals, and warehouses for old age. What cements our slavery to the empire culture is our own fear. We fear of the wilderness. We are afraid of the stranger. Facing our fear is a difficult task when marketing fear is the primary function of most every news program and much of social media. The main journalistic mission is to lead with crime and violence. The news professional and social media thrive on wrongdoing and finding out who is at fault. Every media commercial exploits our belief in scarcity and promises us more security, more power, and more ways to be loved. The bombardment from every direction is intense.

The most difficult part of shifting from the imperial to the neighborly narrative is learning how to question our thinking about charity and social action. We have done a good job of serving the poor, but that is not ending poverty. We will invest any amount of talent and wealth through philanthropy and legislation to increase health services, add classrooms, add police, and put more helping professionals on the frontlines. The paradox, of course, is that the medical profession does fight disease. Schools do help children learn. Police fight crime, treatment centers and case workers help keep people off the street, clothed and fed. Prisons also keep troubled people off the streets. The challenge is that these services have built-in limitations. One limitation is that most of these institutional solutions are run in the imperial way with attention on control, scale, cost, and speed, which is dehumanizing and commodifying to staff and client alike.

The larger limitation, which is a main point of this book, is that the major determinants of health, learning, safety, and well-being reside not in the hands of professionals or organizations or the credentialed elite, but in the relational realm—the network of relationships and the social capital that reside in the hands of our community, and the people in our neighborhoods. The option to empire is community. This is what is missing in finding a place for our hearts and compassion to make a real difference in the economic stability and general well-being of the people on the margins. Wars on poverty, drugs, and violence have produced more of what they were designed to eliminate simply because wars, laws, and fences are the only tools available to the empire mentality.

What will reduce poverty is the will of a neighborhood, combined with its relatedness to the larger community, and a decision to trust each other, which means that neighbors, often led by the faith community, will, first, create an alternative narrative about and relationship with the people we care about. This alternative narrative acknowledges that we have enough. Second, we will then follow that with investment money and access to the support that people who are socially and economically connected—who know about finances, marketing, technology, real estate, and law—take for granted.

We know that the associational life of a neighborhood produces health. We know that what produces a child who learns and is useful and grows into a positive human being is a place where ten people outside the family know the name of that child, and a place where that child has stability in their housing and economic life. We have known for a while that a safe place is created when neighbors have their eyes on the street—a front-yard-and-front-porch-way of being together. We now know that if people who are geographically close trust one another and are willing to work together, they can make the place better. Key in this is the capacity of a neighborhood to welcome strangers. These are the elements of a beloved community. And who better to create these conditions than the faith community—in this book, the Church.

> We no longer divide the human community into friends and others. Instead there are only friends along the way. When we obey God's call to go, there are no strangers or aliens. (p. 7)

This calls for the end of charity, for it divides us from those we claim to care about. Divided from our neighbors, coarsely labeled as the poor, divides us from God

Departing the Empire and Egypt

If the beginning of the transformation of how we bring our faith into the world is to emancipate the internal functioning of the Church from its imperial habits, the next big step is to reimagine what the missional work of the Church might be. How do we invest and work in the neighborhood that is also free from the habits of empire?

As this book calls to us, it begins with acknowledging that the context for this communal neighborly attention is not about traditional political action, social action, or charity. There is tension in almost every faith community about the ideological questions of the day: right to life, same sex marriage, gender equality, gun control, welfare to work, left and right, liberal and conservative, war and peace, climate crisis or denial. These contests in ideology are taking place within the context of the imperial, scarcity, patriarchal narrative. These divisions are territorial claims for dominance in what laws we pass, what voting rights we grant, how we tax each other, and how we determine which boats rise with the tide and which ones sink to the ocean floor.

Of course, these social issues matter, and each of us has a heartfelt point of view about what is best for our family, our local interests, and the larger common good. The harsh reality is that these longstanding points of contention have not ended poverty, improved our health, cared for our children, stabilized the housing of too many of our neighbors. They, in fact, have increased our isolation, our like-mindedness, our addiction to stimulants, and our fear of the stranger.

The same must be said for philanthropy and charity. In addition to the love underlying charity, there is a scarcity and imperial force that declares that other people are needy, perhaps broken, and need us to fix them. To state it perhaps too strongly, if a church takes pride in feeding the poor on a regular basis, as an act of compassion, are people any more in control of their economic lives after dinner than they were before dinner? The call is not to stop the feeding, or clothing, or housing, because the needs are real. The problem is in how we perceive the neighbors we are feeding, clothing, and housing. When we name them poor, we declare them not only broke, but broken. This is seeing the world with the eyes of Pharaoh.

God calls God's people to create a new community of shalom. We must take care not to simply make God's mission into a social ethic or universal morality. God's call is not merely a means for achieving better wages and working conditions for the enslaved. It cannot be narrowly defined as a socio-political intervention or strategy. Shalom community is not limited to "strategies to ensure just distribution of resources, or theories of justice presupposed by such policies."[1] God does not give Moses a theory of justice. God wants to foster very real, transformed, and renewed relationships among the people of Israel and the people of Egypt.

Neighborly Economics and the Beloved Community

The neighborly narrative takes our attention away from the imperial arguing and away from our charitable patterns and puts our attention strictly on the determinants of the well-being of neighbors, which moves the Church into the elimination of poverty, not just serving the poor. That move begins with a change in labeling. There is no such thing as a poor person, or a homeless person, or a troubled youth, or an ex-offender. These labels are too small a version of a human being. They drive solutions that keep us all stuck as strangers. When we see that neighbors are not poor, but are economically isolated, we name an idea we can do something with. We can reduce their isolation by learning who they are and what they are good at, and then invest in their enterprise with a neighborly support system to insure their success. Same with people experiencing homelessness, whom we used to call homeless. We can find out what they are good at, and find ways for them to offer their gifts. Many can cook, pray, sing, listen, live outside, and waste little.

The neighborly narrative calls for joining the movement toward a cooperative economy, based on the common good rather than private, competitive interests. We can take a financial interest in the path of local real estate development so that gentrification is more evenly balanced with investment in locally owned businesses, common land and buildings, and micro start-ups. In this work, we can include the quality of the local environment. We can invest resources in the food hub surrounding the church, caring about where food is grown and how it is distributed and priced. We can commit to finding usefulness for our teenagers, connect our elderly with our children, bring our neighbors with disabilities into the rooms where we meet, or into our storefronts. We can become committed to the connectedness and health of our neighbors. We can enlarge our role as conveners to bring neighbors together to reclaim the commons.

All of these now are attended to by the professionals in health care, public safety, economics, supermarkets and agriculture, education, and government. They do what they can, but they are incapable of effecting true transformation. The real exodus from empire will come from citizens exiting the market ideology and its dependence on professional services and the programs of the charitable industrial complex.

The good news is that none of the transformative alternatives have to be invented. There are social innovations all around us that give us valuable models: the Parish Collective, the Abundant Community Initiative in Edmonton, The Hive in Cincinnati, the neighborhood economics movement called SOCAP, The Jubilee Project Cincinnati, The Jubilee Fund of Cincinnati's Christ Church Cathedral, Oasis, BALLE, Yes! Magazine, Common Change, the Greater Rochester Health Foundation, the Family Independence Initiative. There are many more examples, these are just the ones I am close to. All of these efforts are building connected families and neighborhoods, and most are funneling financial investment and support into residents' hands in economically isolated neighborhoods. They are proof of concept for the ideas in this beautifully constructed book and confirmation that the movement is underway.

The Church has been headed toward these ideas for a while, and many of these efforts have been created out of the missional commitment of churches and church leaders. This book makes this direction clear and compelling. It calls us is to put this vocation front and center as the work of the faith community. It brings the Church full force, in the words of our friend Walter Brueggemann, into our double agency with God.

> God invites and God sends all of God's people. This is not a professional or clerical invitation. God's call to ordinary people undergirds all other work done in God's name. . . . The words to Isaiah echo for us, "Whom will I send? Who will go on my behalf? Who will be my messenger?" It is a not a call to professionals or specialists. God calls all brothers and sisters into new relationships, and a new kingdom of shalom. Who will answer the invitation to go? (p. 12)

Enjoy the book.

Introduction: Selling Jesus

Hence the vocation of the Church of Christ in the world, in political con-
flict and social strife, is inherently eschatological. The Church is the embassy
of the eschaton in the world. The Church is the image of what the world
is in its essential being. The Church is the trustee of the society which the
world, not subjected to the power of death, is to be on that last day when
the world is fulfilled in all things in God.

—William Stringfellow[1]

I believe that God has a mission. God's mission has a church—a
community—and we are that community of beloved apostles. As
such, how do we stop fumbling over institutional trappings and get
to the business of our mission? What are the theological and spiritual
imperatives that mark the work before us? And what are the economies
that force us to rely on outdated models of being and doing church? I
have explored these questions in previous books, sharing the conversations I have been having as a priest and then bishop of the Episcopal
Church with my diocese and beyond. I have come to believe that some
aspects of our formation for the future lie in how the Church functioned
in the past. I believe firmly that there is a great tide that washes through
the Church both from the past and the future. If we look carefully at our
past, we can see the seeds of our own becoming.

I believe that the Holy Spirit draws us forward. Discernment and conversation, cost what they will and lead where they may, are essential for

xxii   INTRODUCTION: SELLING JESUS

leadership and strategy. All of creation flows out of the community of the Divine Trinity and is a reciprocation, a return to God, of this divine gift. We are part of that eternal return. Yet, as an institution filled with people, we also wander adrift, blown by winds that lead us elsewhere (Eph. 4:14). In every age, therefore, we examine the faith we have received in order to make necessary course corrections to ensure that we are traveling with the tide of God's Spirit and not futilely rowing against it.

There is no doubt that we have seen seismic shifts over the past fifty years of Church mission. The givens for discipleship, our assumptions about community norms, and the very economies we depend upon continue to change. Many old forms have become millstones around our necks, and many parts of the Christian Church are gasping for air. At the same time, creativity and hope spring forth as leaders point their people toward a gospel vision outside their church doors. Every day, people attempt new ways of undertaking God's mission. They need our prayers and resources—time, energy, and money. My books and my ministry have attempted to offer some cover for the entrepreneurs, the crazy ones, the misfits, the rebels, the troublemakers, the round pegs, and the ones who see things differently. The tenacious creative people among us are not only where energy for the future can be found; they are also able to show us where the steep learning curves are.

My conversations with people committed to a mission-driven future led me to write *CHURCH, A Generous Community,* and *Small Batch.* As the conversation evolved, I found something was still getting in the way. I wrote *Jesus Heist* after realizing that so many of us within the institution use an institutional lens to read the scriptures. In *Jesus Heist* I offered a new hermeneutic for reading the scripture: a missional perspective. The next challenge is locating the primary work of the Church. After years of working within the institutional Church, many of us know how it does business. But what is the work really for? This book focuses on the vocation of the inherited Church, but not its myriad accouterments. This book asks: What are the Church's vocations? What is the work of the baptized? A Church refocused on mission will never happen without a mass enlivening—a great awakening—of the people of God. William Stringfellow wrote in *An Ethic for Christians and Other Aliens in a Strange Land*:

I am called in the Word of God—as is *everyone* else—to the vocation of being human, nothing more and nothing less. . . . To be a Christian means to be called to be an exemplary human being. And, to be a Christian *categorically* does not mean being religious. Indeed, all religious versions of the gospel are profanities. . . . In the face of death, live humanly. In the middle of chaos, celebrate the Word. Amidst Babel, speak the truth. Confront the noise and verbiage and falsehood of death with the truth and potency and efficacy of the Word of God. Know the Word, teach the Word, nurture the Word, preach the Word, define the Word, incarnate the Word, do the Word, live the Word. And more than that, in the Word of God, expose death and all death's works and wiles, rebuke lies, cast out demons, exorcise, cleanse the possessed, raise those who are dead in mind and conscience.[2]

Somewhere along the great arc of history, the Church abdicated its primary vocation of being God in Christ Jesus's body in the world, and started selling Jesus and eternal life as a consumer product instead. Jesus said, "The kingdom of God has come near" (Mark 1:15). But today, when people experience the Church, do they feel that the kingdom has come near? I fear that many more would say "no" than would say "yes."

Along the way, the Church became a worldly principality. It is often remarked that this churchly kingdom looks much different than the community imagined by Jesus. It is worth inspecting this universe of Church and its centripetal forces carefully. The Church has a very natural way of taking the focus off of Jesus and the scripture and placing it on its own institutional needs. As the influences of the world have pressed in, especially the disciplines of business and organizational culture, all nondenominational and denominational church leaders have begun to make matters other than the gospel the lens by which they lead. Far too often, I succumb to this temptation in my own ministry. I know how challenging it can be to make mission primary, and I find that when it comes to vocation, this is doubly true. We can trace the history of vocation to see how this institutional bait-and-switch happened and where this churchly kingdom is presently headed.

xxiv   INTRODUCTION: SELLING JESUS

This book will challenge us to acknowledge that the vocations of the Church are not meant to protect God behind an impermeable screen of holiness. Such protective behaviors serve our own interest and that of the institutional kingdom—at the expense of Jesus. In order to grasp the future of vocational life, we must learn to see Christ working in the world and through others.

As we ponder the future of the Church's vocation and the vocations of its members, we ought to be curious about the emerging mission work of the baptized. This is essential. We now face a mission age. We must start Christian communities that are not priestly or institutionally oriented. We must help people discern their calling in the world and on behalf of God. And we must also increase ordinations (because of retirements) while asking, "What kind of ordinands will we raise up?" We must make more ways of training available to both the baptized and clergy, but how? We must get curious about what processes for discerning clergy leadership work, but are all clergy formed the same way? Furthermore, the discernment of lay vocations cannot be an afterthought, simply for those turned down by leadership for the ordained ministry. Lay vocations should be our *first* thought. Some may discover a call to be ordained, but most will find an enlivened sense of themselves and their community as part of the baptized.

We have been focused liturgically on the recovery of the central role of baptism within our churches and liturgy. The twentieth century was an age of defining the rules of the assembly. During the high watermark of parochial ministry, we spent a vast amount of theological and corporate energy defining baptism in the midst of the Eucharist. Then, we quibbled about *what* language best incorporated the baptized into the communal celebration, which resulted in numerous trial liturgies and a new prayer book in 1979. Our older generation of leaders now long for another revision before their time passes, but face a church weary of change. We have also spent a good amount of resources sorting out who is allowed to celebrate in the community. Who can be a deacon, a priest, or bishop? Can the celebrant be a woman? Can they be a priest but not a bishop? Can they be gay? Transgender? Single? Or Divorced? These have been the questions about the assembly that occupied our liturgical efforts in the past century.

Other questions remain unanswered. For instance, the baptized might ask, "Am I participating as the priest prays, or is the priest praying my prayer? Are the clergy praying with us or for us?" The questions point to the hierarchy of orders. Is the priest one of us as we pray the Eucharistic prayer together? Is the priest our chosen celebrant among equals with the baptized? Or is the priest praying the prayer for the congregation? The latter suggests a hierarchy where the priestly vocation is to pray on behalf of the baptized. The Rt. Rev. Neil Alexander, bishop and dean of the School of Theology at Sewanee, has a helpful way of thinking about the complex work of the Church in these conversations. He says, "Every time we move our theological thinking in one area, we move everything else in relationship to it. It is all like a mobile."[3] When you pull on the vocation of the baptized, it moves the ordinal, and moves our ecclesiology. Historically, the assembled congregation (one priest, one church building, Sunday morning services, one plot of land, and an internally focused ministry) has dominated every part of our theology, ecclesiology, and liturgy for a century. Moreover, the primary actors in that space and dialogue have been the clergy, and priests most of all.

Our parochial orientation has affected our every move, and has been a stumbling block to engaging mission. Due to the high place liturgy has played in this discourse, we have completely left the questions of mission, and the formation of the baptized for that mission, off the table. In fact, it has been argued that liturgy *is* mission. However, a church that focuses most of its time, energy, and resources on Sunday morning liturgy is not missional. The professionalizing of the priesthood and Episcopacy has diminished lay orders, robbing laypeople of their external mission work, and leaving them to spiritually tend to the most basic of ministries that revolve around Sunday morning activities. Many generations of the baptized have been spiritually transformed by their stewardship for the sake of a temple-oriented tradition and ministry at the Lord's altar.[4] But the work of the Church is not limited to an altar-centered faith alone. The baptized during this age have been particularly resilient and their faith has led them to start, build, and discover new forms of ministry outside the confines of the institutional Church. They have adapted to the changing

shape of culture and formed nonprofit and nongovernmental organizations to undertake their vocations of service. Many have left the building
and have not returned. The Church has not followed them into these mission adventures to support, learn, and share.

Given the short shrift the baptized have received over the last few
decades, we must, in fact, begin with laypeople instead of tacking them onto
the end of a discussion of vocations. The uncomfortable truth for the institutional Church is that missional vitality combined with the shared Episcopal
DNA of the baptized will be the key to a healthy future. In my diocese,
there is a very old family business. The great-grandsons of the organization's
founder manage it today. Their immigrant story, along with their partnership
with the church, is an essential piece of the corporation's DNA. They have
had to work to create a method of transferring the corporate family DNA,
entrusting the future of their business methods and activities to new generations of employees. The same kinds of formation will have to be adapted to
our use as we become a mission-minded community of the baptized at work
in the world, supported by the clergy orders and one another.

We will need to discern and develop baptismal vocations that help
people go out from the Church to serve the world and start new communities in God's name. We must seek to understand how we got to a
place where the empowerment of the baptized always pointed to discernment for priesthood. We must confess that we have given lip service to the
baptized while overemphasizing a false hierarchy focused on perpetuating clerical ministry. Our focus on discernment, seminaries, ordination,
and internal parochial life and liturgy has sidelined discussions around the
formation of God's people. As Bishop Alexander cautions us, any discussion about vocations will affect everything. We must be courageous as we
proceed, because our task is monumental—we must imagine the future of
baptismal vocation for mission. We must plumb the depths of the Church's
vocation, its reason for being, and its means of participating in God's mission. Like an Alexander Calder mobile, when we tug on mission and the
baptized as part of that work, all the other parts of the Church will move.
The chief occupation of any discussion about the future of vocations must
have two key components of the mobile in play at all times: the vocation of

the Church itself and the formation of the baptized for that mission. Only by holding these two things closely together can we pull apart our myopic and internally focused hermeneutic.

Not long ago I was getting coffee at my favorite coffee shop. The young man making my coffee and I have had several conversations about faith and religion. On this day he asked me, "So what do you think about the Catholic Church?"

I asked him to clarify, as I had a lot of opinions and it was a big topic. He simply offered that he did not think it looked much like what Jesus imagined. I told him he was right and that neither did we as Episcopalians. I said that, as a bishop, I thought we should be responsive to his question. In every missional age, I said, reformation is invited and even called for. The Church as the living body of Christ is out in the world at work. This is happening through the prophets, teachers, and people who minister from underneath the shadow of the Church. If the Church is to be like Christ, it must go out and join people where the work is being done. Only then will it truly be the body of Christ. He agreed and I think he was curious about what that might look like. We will have to have more conversations to be sure. He seems faithful, concerned, and curious about the future shape of ministry, and by that I mean the ministry of people in Jesus's name.

The Church has often sought to protect itself from its instinctive curiosity and from the uncertain nature of sharing the burden of ministry with those who are not members. It was true at the time of Moses's ministry. We find in Numbers 11:27 that Eldad and Medad were prophesying on God's behalf, which was seen as a challenge to Moses's authority, and so a young man came to tattle. Jacob asked Moses to make them stop. Moses said, "Are you jealous for my sake? Would that all the LORD's people were prophets, and that the LORD would put his spirit on them!" (v. 29).

The same of course happened with Jesus. In Mark 9:38, we are told that the disciples were sent out to do Jesus's work. They came back to tell Jesus about their success. But they said they saw people "casting out demons" in Jesus's name, and they were scandalized because those people were not part of the group Jesus sent out. They told Jesus they tried to stop the rogue exorcists because they were not part of the in-crowd. Jesus's response was much like Moses's. He said, "Do not stop them." They were part of his ministry if they chose to do it in his name.

The people who love God the most often get confused and think they need to protect God. But as Jesus teaches, sometimes it is actually these followers who must be renewed by what they see and experience in outsiders. Sometimes salt loses its flavor (Mark 9:50). Our work is to reject the desire to protect God and our ministry from others, and to reimagine the vocation of those who call themselves followers of God in Christ Jesus.

After reading my book *The Jesus Heist*, the Rev. Rebecca Stevens, chaplain at Vanderbilt University's St. Augustine's Chapel in Nashville and founder of Thistle Farms, said, "So what happens if we take your words seriously? Will there be no bishops?" Maybe. But I doubt it. I think the institutional Church is here to stay. What I hear us saying in our conversations is: We are out here doing God's work. It is not enough to change the structures of Church and orient them around mission. The very people who do that work will have to change and be transformed to undertake mission differently. Space must be given to people to do mission in a safe way. Lay missionaries must be able to engage the culture knowing that bishops, priests, and deacons are supporting them.

We have invested in the setting apart of leaders and ordaining people in a system and culture that is loyal to an old model of church. Stevens is right. We must change not only where we go and what we do; we must also change who we are and how we choose and train our leaders. Perhaps the way deacons, priests, and bishops work will need to be different in the future. Maybe, in fact, just as we have sought to understand the mission of the Church differently, we should ask ourselves about the ministers of the Church. If we dare to call ourselves "Christ's Body" and undertake the work of going where Christ went, and doing what Christ did, and hanging out with the people Christ hung out with, then maybe we should pray God give us wisdom to become the people doing this work. Maybe we should ask God to open up the living word of scripture and invite us to see the work of God's people in a new light, outside the ministry of church structure and institution. The question before us as an institutional Church is *not* "How will we save the Church?" Instead, the questions are:

How will we work with people to find their call to serve the world? What are the different roles needed in this new missional age? And what parts of our organization need to be reshaped to help us accomplish this work together? We are even now writing the story of this generation's response to the gospel. What is before us are mission-shaped vocations.

CHAPTER ONE

A Shalom Making God

God's call disrupts the lives of settled people, both in biblical times and now. God sends, then and now, to transform the present world, subject to alien powers, into the world God intends. Discipleship and evangelism are, therefore, not primarily about church membership and recruitment but about an alternative way of being in the world for the sake of the world.
—Walter Brueggemann[1]

God calls people to be about God's work. The call is neither complicated nor hidden from view. On the other hand, religion calls priests. Religion redacts scripture to find traces of contemporary priesthood models to support a temple/church-oriented system. As we look at the whole of scripture without the lens of institution to misguide us, we see God calling people into God's work and mission. When we include the Old Testament into this picture, we see important typologies that are echoed in the New Testament. God's Spirit has been at work before time began and throughout time as we know it. God's call to our ancient faith ancestors, therefore, is constant and consistent in manner and form with God's call through the Incarnate Word and the Holy Spirit in the New Testament. Our sense of our own calling must begin with curiosity about how God has called God's people from the very beginning, because the vocations held within the Church are not simply vocations of a "New Testament" kind, but are rooted in the authority of the patriarchs and matriarchs of Israel.

In the Old Testament, God calls a wide variety of people. God calls Israel into the wilderness and invites them to give of themselves. In the wilderness they ask, "Did you bring us out here to die?" The answer to all of God's people throughout scripture, and to our communities today, is, "Yes." We are constantly invited by God to leave the comfort of our lives for the discomfort of the journey with God.[2] God is at work for the world itself. To redeem the world is God's mission. God calls people into community for the purpose of redemption: the inauguration of the kingdom of God. This emerging kingdom causes friction and is always in conflict with the culture of humanity and, oftentimes, the Church. We can see this throughout the circumstances of biblical history and in our own context.

Whole books could be written that detail the various invitations God made to this or that person in the Old Testament. There are the creation stories and God's invitation to Adam and Eve to work in the Garden. There is the calling of Noah to restart creation. Abram (Abraham) and Sarai (Sarah) are called to leave the land of Ur of the Chaldeans—the beginning of generations of God's people. There are the judges and the prophets. Jacob is called and renamed. There are women: Miriam—a leader who brings Israel out of slavery in Egypt with Moses; Deborah—a judge of Israel; Huldah—a prophetess who helped Josiah; Ruth and Naomi; and Esther—the queen of Persia, to name a few. The sheer number of called people is too many to number, but we will examine a few of these crucial stories.

Let us begin with Abraham and Sarah, originally called Abram and Sarai and renamed for their faithfulness. In many ways the story of their calling begins the narrative of God's people. Abraham and Sarah were frequently cited by the early Church as examples of God's expansive promise to all people. God said, "Go," and all of their worldly plans were set aside as they left their homeland for God's wilderness. Their lives were disrupted by God's invitation and their response. Theologian Walter Brueggemann says Abraham is caught up in a world of discourse and possibility about which he knew nothing until addressed, a world of discourse and possibility totally saturated with God's good promises for him and for the world through him (Gen 12:1). By this call Abraham is propelled into an orbit of reality that totally preempts his life and removes him completely from any purpose or agenda he may have entertained for himself before that moment.[3]

Abraham and Sarah offered themselves faithfully to the journey and became a blessing to the world.

The same invitation was given to Moses, Esther, and Jonah. God sent Moses to Pharaoh to speak on God's behalf. God invited Moses onto holy ground and challenged him to accept the mission of freeing God's people. Accepting the invitation meant that Moses would leave his past life behind: his journey in Egypt, the murder he committed, his fleeing into the pasturelands, and his long exile shepherding sheep. God invited Moses to join in the long line of ancestors on God's mission of shalom—of peace. Brueggemann says that Moses's call was "an abrupt act that displaces Moses for a world of conflict propelled by God's holiness."[4] Moses was oblivious to the long history of God's mission until he stood on that holy ground and was invited to "go" on God's behalf. Like Abraham and Sarah, his *going* was about bringing a blessing to the world. Vocation is broader than being called into community. Vocation is also about acceding to God's disruptive mission—saying "yes," and then going.[5]

Esther, the queen of Persia, was called by God and given work to do. In a departure from how God dealt with Moses and Abraham, God did not come to Esther directly, but spoke to her through others. While the means may be different, God's invitation was the same. Haman had a plan for King Xerxes to annihilate all of the Jews in the kingdom, and Esther was the agent of protection for God's people. It was Mordecai, Esther's cousin, who first spoke to Esther about the plight of her people in Esther 2:7, and she was immediately brought into the conflict.

Through Mordecai, God invited Esther to "go" and plead with Xerxes not to carry out Haman's plan (Esther 4:8). Esther resisted God's invitation delivered through Mordecai. Mordecai then said, "For if you keep silence at such a time as this, relief and deliverance will rise for the Jews from another quarter, but you and your father's family will perish. Who knows? Perhaps you have come to royal dignity for just such a time as this" (Esther 4:14). Mordecai reframed Esther's royal standing as an opportunity, an invitation into the greater story of God and God's people. Despite her fearful preoccupations about safety, God invited Esther to enter the plight of her people. She was to be a blessing to the world by stopping the king's violence and saving her people.

Isaiah's call story is commonly read at Episcopal ordination services today. We do not know much about Isaiah. He was one of the great prophets and a school, or guild, continued to prophesy in his name after his death. We do know that Isaiah began his career immediately following King Uzziah's death. Uzziah, whose name means "Yahweh is my strength," was evidently an excellent king of Judah. He brought the military to great victories and built forts and towers. He fostered development in the fields of agriculture and trade (2 Chron. 26). He did everything right in God's sight (2 Chron. 27:2). And he had leprosy. The scripture tells us he was prideful and was not the best at worshipping God. He was rarely seen in the temple. But he was beloved and the nation was strong. When Uzziah died, everything changed and Judah was beset by adversity. Under threat economically and militarily, the very safety of God's people was jeopardized by surrounding enemies.

In the midst of this sea change, Isaiah was called. Abraham heard God's voice, Moses heard God speak from a bush, and Esther heard God speak through Mordecai. Isaiah's calling was inaugurated by a great vision.

> In the year that King Uzziah died, I saw the Lord sitting on a throne, high and lofty; and the hem of his robe filled the temple. Seraphs were in attendance above him; each had six wings: with two they covered their faces, and with two they covered their feet, and with two they flew. And one called to another and said:
> "Holy, holy, holy is the LORD of hosts;
> the whole earth is full of his glory."

The pivots on the thresholds shook at the voices of those who called, and the house filled with smoke. (Isa. 6:1–4)

Esther was afraid to honor God's call because it put her at risk. Moses had other plans and believed he could not speak well enough to accomplish what God wished. Isaiah suffered no such ambivalence. He humbly accepted God's invitation, believing that he was not worthy to go for God because he was unclean. God sent one of the creatures down and touched Isaiah's lips with a burning coal taken from the altar. Then God asked, "Whom shall I send? Who will be my messenger?" God invited Isaiah to respond. Isaiah answered, "I will go! Send me!" (Isa. 6:6–8). Again, it was an invitation to go—an invitation that overwhelmed misgivings about worthiness, personal plans for the future, or bodily safety.

Finally, there is the story of Jonah. I mention Jonah because he flat out rejected God's invitation at first. God asked Jonah to go to Nineveh. Jonah's response was to go to Tarshish. He went to Joppa, got on a boat, and attempted to flee from God's call. A storm came up, the sailors threw Jonah overboard, a big fish swallowed him, and then, upon being spit up on the shore, Jonah heard God again: "Get up, go to Nineveh, that great city, and proclaim to it the message that I tell you." Jonah went to Nineveh to be God's messenger (Jon. 1–3).

The reason that Jonah did not want to go was because God was too forgiving! Jonah knew that if he did what God wanted, then God would simply forgive the people. Jonah complained angrily when God proved him right. He cried out in prayer, "O Lord! Is not this what I said while I was still in my own country? That is why I fled to Tarshish at the beginning; for I knew that you are a gracious God and merciful, slow to anger, and abounding in steadfast love, and ready to relent from punishing" (Jon. 4:2).

God's invitations are very persuasive. Through visions, voice, and the advice and counsel of friends, God invites God's people to *go*. The specific circumstances of this *going* vary across different contexts, but there is always purpose behind God's invitation to *go*. People are always being *sent*. There is a hinge here in the language—a double meaning: going and being sent are about both the invitation and the purpose.

God called Abraham and Sarah to become a people that bless the world, which is a habit of God's throughout all of scripture. Faithfulness is the act of accepting the invitation and opening oneself to becoming the blessing. Those whom God invites, God also blesses, in order that they might bless others. God said to Abraham and Sarah, "In you all the families of the earth shall be blessed" (Gen. 12:3). Their promised family would outnumber the stars of Abraham's counting and be a blessing to the world. Brueggemann ponders the meaning of this blessing and says, "'Blessing' is not a religious or moral phenomenon in the world," it is a "characteristic feature of creation that is fruitful and productive."[6]

Creation was separated from God because its communal structures were organized around itself as opposed to God. These inwardly focused structures perpetuated a mimesis, a repetition, of violence that created a dark shadow over the kingdom of God. Abraham and Sarah were called to show how human community could be different. God made a point of rejecting religious violence by refusing Abraham's offer of Isaac as a sacrifice. God undid the human drive to sanctify murder. God was interested in a shalom that broke the repetitive, violent cycle of Cain and Abel. Abraham and Sarah's call was to heal the violence that separated humanity from God. Yet, the feud continues, and so does the division between God and humanity.

Even with all of religion's great gifts to society, we must acknowledge that disunity and tribal grievances still exist. God continues to invite us to go as peace bearers and we continue, often, to reject the invitation. It is religion that calls for the sacrifice of Jesus. His is one name among the many who have been scapegoated for the sake of political and religious peace. Religions have a propensity to scapegoat others. God's invitation to Abraham and Sarah was an invitation beyond this history of sacrifice. God went further and sent the peace bearers to dwell in the midst of the other.

The relationship between Abraham and God is typological of God's relationship with all whom God invites into mission. Abraham was invited to be in community with God, and to take that community on the road. God's call removes us from the realm of self-definition: we begin to define ourselves as creatures in relationship with our Creator. This movement dissolves the idea of the "other," for the only true other is God. We no longer divide the human community into friends and others. Instead, there are only friends along the way. When we obey God's call to go, there are no strangers or aliens. Chief Rabbi Jonathan Sacks writes that our invitation to journey with God means confessing and rejecting the notion that

> for there to be an "us" there must be a "them," the people not like us. Humanity is divided into friends and strangers, brothers and others. The people not like us become the screen onto which we project our fears. They are seen as threatening, hostile, demonic. Identity involves exclusion which leads to violence.[7]

To journey as Abraham and Sarah did is to reject our inclination to protect ourselves by force. In their going—in our going—we embrace our vulnerability and forsake our tribe in order to journey with God and God's tribe, pronouncing God's blessing upon the world. Brueggemann says, "Abraham is called to exist so that the general condition of curse in the world is turned to a general condition of blessing, life, and well-being. Israel's mission is to mend the world in all its parts." God's people are to be a blessing in the world. God intends the world to be "generous, abundant, and fruitful, effecting generative fertility, material abundance, and this-worldly prosperity—*shalom* in the broadest scope."[8]

The importance of being a people bringing about peace and blessing in the world is affirmed in the teaching of the early Church. Paul used God's call to Abraham and Sarah and their blessing as a paradigm of the expanding mission of God. Paul read the blessing and invitation of God as being fulfilled in the great expansion of grace to all people regardless of ethnicity, gender, and social class (Gal. 3:8). God will not be limited to a religious or ethnic "us vs. them," but instead imagines a kingdom where we are all beloved of God. This kingdom is founded upon the rejection of violence for the sake of nation, and faith in favor of shalom for God. Our presence and participation in God's creation is our invitation into the community of blessing—this community of shalom. We are rooted in it by our very nature. The mission is not about nation-states, or making people members of religious institutions; the mission is a journey into a new community of being.

While God sent Abraham and Sarah as a blessing to the whole world, God sent Moses as a blessing of peace and a means of deliverance for God's people. Egypt had become an intolerably ugly place for master and slave alike, and God intervened in this evil course of affairs by sending Moses. Egypt was supported by slave labor long before the Israelites ever arrived. The pyramid of Giza was built before the birth of Abraham.

> When life becomes cheap and people are seen as a means not an end, when the worst excesses are excused in the name of tradition and rulers have absolute power, then conscience is eroded and freedom lost because the culture has created insulated space in which the cry of the oppressed can no longer be heard.[9]

We already know that enslaving one another is part of the cycle of violence. The enslavement of God's people in Egypt was even prophesied to Abraham when he began his journey. Abraham and Sarah's people were destined to be strangers in a strange land.[10] Regardless of his plan to live out his days shepherding with his father-in-law, Jethro, Moses was sent to bring shalom to the people in Egypt.

God said, "I have observed the misery of my people who are in Egypt; I have heard their cry on account of their taskmasters. Indeed, I know their sufferings, and I have come down to deliver them from the Egyptians. . . . The cry of the Israelites has now come to me; I have also seen how the Egyptians oppress them" (Exod. 3:7–9). Brueggemann points out that God often goes and does this or that. However, in the call stories, God sends someone as an envoy. In this case, God sent Moses.[11] God said to Moses, "So come, I will send you to Pharaoh to bring my people, the Israelites, out of Egypt" (v. 10).

This is an important part of God's shalom-making. Throughout scripture, we see God at work, reconciling the world to God's self. God is also at work building and recreating the world into the kingdom of peace or shalom: the realm of God. God does this work by reversing the world founded upon violent human interaction. God does not reverse a world of violent human interaction alone; this is work that humans must do by God's invitation. We might say it this way: God could come down and free God's people alone. Instead, God acts with humanity. God acted with Moses to deliver a new state of being to Egypt and the Israelites. It was to be a new relationship. Of course, the Egyptians were not be able to live within this new relationship without paying a considerable cost in terms of life and wealth. God sent Moses into a real political world. He went into a real context bisected by powers, authorities, and human-made kingdoms of violence.[12] As Stanley Hauerwas is fond of saying, "Faith is not a private matter." To live into God's call, Moses could not hide in the mountains where his sheep grazed. The God who spoke from the fiery bush sends those whom God calls into the world of violent, enslaving powers.

We are part of this history. We are part of God's call to Moses. We bear witness to a God who raised Jesus Christ after first raising the people of Israel out of Egypt. We are to be "a sign that God has not abandoned the world."[13] God's "work"—God's "vocation"—is outside of the world's powers, and different from the way these powers work. Moreover, God's shalom can only be enacted in person, in community between human beings. Our society stands against this notion of God's "sending" work—this community of shalom. We reject God's invitation and refuse to go. We prefer to articulate God's shalom as a form of sanctified political activism instead. The invitation to Moses, as with Esther, Isaiah, and Jonah, was no mere political activism. God invites us into a real community where political modes of speech have no purchase. There are political implications to shalom, but for those who accept God's invitation, the journey quickly becomes about a community and a narrative that resonate far more deeply than any political tribalism. God's typology, God's paradigmatic way of inviting and sending, cannot be about clericalism alone, nor can it be about any singular social theory.[14]

God calls God's people to create a new community of shalom. We must take care not to simply make God's mission into a social ethic or universal morality. God's call is not merely a means for achieving better wages and working conditions for the enslaved. It cannot be narrowly defined as a sociopolitical intervention or strategy. Shalom community is not limited to "strategies to ensure just distribution of resources, or the theories of justice presupposed by such policies."[15] God did not give Moses a theory of justice. God wanted to foster real, transformed, and renewed relationships among the people of Israel and the people of Egypt. Remember, the story of Israel in the land of Egypt began with friendship between a lost son and a ruler, Pharaoh and Joseph. What is broken by Israel's slide into slavery is that original relationship. A time had come when people did not remember the blessings they have been for one another. Shalom, peace, is not a political "symbol" or "myth," but a real action of relationship that has a communal/social function in building a different kind of kingdom than the reign of humanity.[16]

If we are to deepen our understanding of the work—the vocation—of the people of God in the future Church, we must come to terms with the fact that we are called to be a community that is completely different from the world around us. Our vocation is not rooted in an historic Church institution, but deeply woven into the fabric of God's creation itself. It is nothing less than the peaceable kingdom. We are not called to make our world or nation better. We need to rethink our posture toward the global sociopolitical institutions that depend on violence, power, and authority. Stanley Hauerwas says:

> Put as directly as I can, it is not the task of the church to try to develop social theories or strategies to make America work; rather the task of the church in this country is to become a polity that has the character necessary to survive as a truthful society. That task carried out would represent a distinctive contribution to the body politic we call America.[17]

I would simply add that these sociopolitical forces have globalized.

We know that inaugurating God's shalom community will be deadly and costly because of the stubbornness of Pharaoh and all of Pharaoh's present-day analogues. Nevertheless, the work of Moses was to be a messenger of shalom to the power of Egypt. Moses was the face of God in the world of violence and oppression. He was the face of God to Pharaoh. Through Moses, God intervened in the world of humans and came into direct conflict with political power. Likewise the call to Esther was to keep the king from committing a Jewish genocide. God directed Isaiah and Jonah to care for the least, the lost, and the suffering—people the rulers of their days had forgotten. They were given the gift of prophesy to invite repentance. God calls us to transform human interaction in profoundly costly ways.

In Egypt, God's shalom expended and exhausted Pharaoh's power. Esther had to expend all her capital and use all her wiles to persuade the king of Persia. Isaiah was destined to grapple with the corrupt powers of Judah who had forgotten God's beloved poor. Jonah was sent into the teeth of the city of Nineveh to preach repentance. All of these people engaged others in costly ways to bring about shalom. God's part was to support them in their mission.

God offers presence, power, wisdom, comfort, and does mighty acts to aid those engaged in the work of shalom making. Brueggemann says that such acts of God can only be "available in the midst of alternative human action."[18] Every person, called and sent, brings about new governance, a new way of being. God uses all of these patriarchs and matriarchs, and many more like them, to inaugurate this new way of being.

This new way of being is God's peaceable kingdom. At the very core of each of the call stories examined above is a new polity, a new politic, grounded on something deeper than violence. Since the very beginning of Genesis, God has been undoing humanity's endless sibling rivalries and inviting us into a community of peace. These sibling rivalries, and the institutions they have birthed, are at the core of human violence.[19] Being called and sent is about participating in a virtuous community of peace. Those who are called and sent do not sacrifice others to satisfy their own wants and desires. Such peace is at the heart of the community Jesus imagined. Such peace is at the heart of eternal communion with God, stretching back to our earliest journeys with God. This peace and its community, its politic, are the means by which all other communities, nations, and politics are to be compared and judged. It is true that we have not always been at our best as the Church, but the fact of our own brokenness should not discourage us from pursuing the kingdom of peace, nor does it excuse us from our holy vocation. As Hauerwas says, "The fact that we have often been less than we were meant to be should never be used as an excuse for shirking the task of being the people of God."[20]

God invites and God sends all of God's people. This is not a professional or clerical invitation. God's call to ordinary people undergirds all other work done in God's name. The core of everything else the Church does is peaceful human interconnectivity. Decisions about who will do what are marginal. The most important thing the Church does is hear God's voice of shalom. This calling finds its first home in ordinary people living ordinary lives. After all, Moses and Esther were not trained to speak to the rulers of their world. Creating the community of shalom is not a professional exercise. There is no financial or economic benefit to any of those whom God calls. God calls the ordinary, unprepared, and often tentative to be God's voice and to create a new world in God's name. There is certainly no safety guaranteed in this work. We must take care not to read back into these call stories the credentialed authority of the modern professional, or the erratic genius of the postmodern technological revolutionary. Heeding God's call is not an economic exchange. There is no room for the prosperity gospel here. Looking back into these stories and making them into a legitimization of the priesthood or a defense of clericalism perverts these texts by reading them through the lens of modern religious systems. Such systems are not implicit in these narratives. The God of Sinai invites the Church to share the burden of this new shalom society equally amongst all her members (Exod. 18:13–27). Everyone has a share in the peaceable kingdom.

The powers and authorities of this world are "alien" to God's desired kingdom of shalom.[21] We are invited to risk the walk with God, and to relate to each other in ways that transform the present moments we experience. The faithful who say yes to God's invitation set aside their plans and die to self so God can undertake mighty works through our relationships. The words to Isaiah echo for us, "Whom will I send? Who will go on my behalf? Who will be my messenger?" It is a not a call to professionals or specialists. God calls all brothers and sisters into new relationships, and a new kingdom of shalom. Who will answer the invitation to go? Who will be willing to be the one sent?

CHAPTER TWO

The Prince of Peace

God was turning the world upside down by choosing her in her littleness. If God can chose someone as ordinary as me to bear the divine into the world, then we better be ready to be surprised where the divine is coming from. . . . Why would God choose a teenage girl? It is just mind blowing.
—Richard Rohr[1]

The New Testament picks up where the Old Testament leaves off, proclaiming God's reign of shalom breaking into the world, beginning with God's invitation to Mary. God spoke to Mary through a messenger: the angel Gabriel (Luke 1:26). Gabriel spoke to Mary with a word most often translated as "greeting" in this passage, but elsewhere in the New Testament the same word is translated as "grace."[2] The angel said, "Grace to you." The angel blessed Mary so that she might be a blessing, as Abraham and Sarah were a blessing. This word for "grace" and "greeting" is also used in the letter to the Hebrews to describe Abraham as a blessing. Elsewhere in the Gospels it refers to the coming of the kingdom. From the very beginning of God's conversation with Mary, we see God's shalom work. God invited Mary into it.

Not unlike her faith ancestors before her, Mary was concerned for herself. Most translations say she was "troubled" by the angel's greeting. The implication is that Mary was concerned about her personal safety. As in the Old Testament, the appearance of God's messenger is a sign that Mary was setting out on God's costly, risky mission. The angel told her not to be afraid because she was to be a "blessing." Gabriel then told her that her womb had received a son whom she was to name Jesus. Mary declared that she will be the "servant" of God. This word is often translated "handmaid," which flattens and impoverishes Luke's intended meaning. Mary was saying that she would indeed serve God's mission. She would be a servant by participating in the work of shalom that God had invited her into. She said, "Let it be done."

Mythical stories of gods copulating with mortal women abound, each resulting in the birth of a hero. In fact, such stories were common in Greece and Rome, the two cultural centers during Mary's time. In these mythical narratives, one of the gods of the Greco-Roman pantheon forces himself upon a mortal woman. Modern retellings of these tales often elide or obscure these implications of rape, but such was not the case in the first century when Luke wrote his Gospel. The Christian philosopher of religion René Girard calls these Greco-Roman narratives "monstrous births of mythology."[3] The mating of the gods with mortals was a violent oppression by a dominating power, undertaken by the gods and then repeated throughout the social orders of Hellenistic humanity. The story of Mary's invitation and acceptance to serve God's mission parallels these stories but also turns them on their heads. Mary's call narrative rejects violence by gods in favor of the peace of God. Girard writes:

> No relationship of violence exists between those who take part in the virgin birth: the Angel, the Virgin and the Almighty. . . . In fact, all the themes and terms associated with the virgin birth convey to us a perfect submission to the non-violent will of the God of the gospels, who in this way prefigures Christ himself.[4]

There was no violence to Mary. She was the lost and least and is raised up. There was no scandal. Mary did not resist her calling. There was no rape or sexual power that overtook her.[5]

More recently, artists have portrayed the overshadowing of Mary as a kind of sexual ecstasy, but these interpretations say more about us than they do about Luke or Mary. The other modern trend, which is to "demythologize" Mary's experience by arguing that Luke has derived her calling narrative from those other more monstrous mythologies, misses the point. When we remove the mystery of God's invitation and Mary's acceptance and flatten Luke's narrative into an unremarkable recapitulation of Greek myth, we remove the message of shalom that is woven into the story of the Incarnation from the outset. When we deconstruct Luke's story and allow our modern sensibilities about science to overshadow it, we make Luke's Gospel into just another story. Bishop John Spong rejected Mary's call narrative as worthless mythology. Paul Tillich had no interest in the mythic birth of Jesus. The story of God's invitation and Mary's willingness to serve is significant precisely in the ways it differs from the pagan stories of monstrous birth, in the ways that the birth narrative departs from the domination culture of antiquity, and the ways is stands in contrast to modernity. The story's rejection of violence is one of the reasons the early Church struggled to achieve legitimacy with Greco-Roman society. God and the conception narrative of Jesus do not adhere to any of the mythic tropes known to paganism, and undermine all such tropes with a story of shalom. Our own sexually oriented culture, also consumed by violence, rejects the story too. God soundly refuses to appease the violent expectations of either epoch.

If we had any remaining doubt about the radical message of peace that Mary entered into, her visit with Elizabeth should dispel it. In the home of Elizabeth, who was to give birth to John the Baptist, we hear Mary speak about the invitation to participate in the reign of shalom that was about to be undertaken by God through her ministry as God-bearer: *Theotokos*. Following in the footsteps of Moses and Esther, who brought about dramatic social change, and Abraham, who was the first to be a blessing, and Isaiah and Jonah, who offered transformation to estranged people, Mary was taking part in God's work of shalom by inaugurating cosmic change.

Mary told Elizabeth that she was humbled, and that God had invited her into the work of being blessed and being a blessing to the world. Perhaps reflecting upon the words of Hannah in 1 Samuel 2:1–11, Mary said that God's mighty acts throughout salvation history had benefited her personally and now she was part of the narrative. Remembering the words of Jonah, we hear her repeat that God was a God of mercy and quick to forgive. Mary said that God raised up the least, the lost, and the lowly. God laid low the powers and authorities of this world. God fed people good things. Those who wish for the ways of the world, the human ways of rivalry and greed, to prevail, would find the gospel of grace difficult and would be sent away empty. This was the reign of shalom. This was a new chapter in the promise God invited Abraham and Sarah into. Mary was to be a part of the great narrative of God, bringing God's blessing of peace into the world. From Luke's first chapter beginning at the forty-sixth verse:

My soul magnifies the Lord,
and my spirit rejoices in God my Savior,
for he has looked with favor on the lowliness of his servant.
Surely, from now on all generations will call me blessed;
for the Mighty One has done great things for me,
and holy is his name.
His mercy is for those who fear him
from generation to generation.
He has shown strength with his arm;
he has scattered the proud in the thoughts of their hearts.
He has brought down the powerful from their thrones,
and lifted up the lowly;
he has filled the hungry with good things,
and sent the rich away empty.
He has helped his servant Israel,
in remembrance of his mercy,
according to the promise he made to our ancestors,
to Abraham and to his descendants for ever.

Many call Mary's song the most concise statement of the gospel. It is a statement of God's vision for a community raised up from the least, the lost, and the lonely. It is a vision of a reign that comes in peace and rejects any kingdom, nation, or state made from violence. It is such a radical statement of God's in-breaking peace that it has come to be feared by the powers and authorities of this world. Mary's song tells of a God who will overthrow the various states that humanity so violently brings into being. Mary's song has repeatedly been outlawed because it threatens the violent structures of human power. Anglicans join the Roman Church in appreciation for Mary's song, called the *Magnificat* in Latin. The states supported by Anglican Churches have not always been so appreciative, however. When India was ruled by the British, the recitation of the *Magnificat* in worship was outlawed. The same was true in Guatemala during the 1980s. Believing that the song of Mary was a rallying cry for the revolutionary and the poor, the government banned it. Guatemala was one of the first countries to practice forced disappearances—between forty and fifty thousand people were summarily murdered in this way. In South America, after the "disappearing" of many family members and children during the dirty war in Argentina, the Mothers of the Plaza de Mayo (a square in the Montserrat barrio of central Buenos Aires) placed the words of the *Magnificat* on posters in the city. The military junta of Argentina responded by banning all public displays of the song for five years.[6] Protestant theologian and activist during Hitler's Germany, Dietrich Bonheoffer, wrote from prison in 1933:

> The song of Mary is the oldest Advent hymn. It is at once the most passionate, the wildest, one might even say the most revolutionary Advent hymn ever sung. This is not the gentle, tender, dreamy Mary whom we sometimes see in paintings. . . . This song has none of the sweet, nostalgic, or even playful tones of some of our Christmas carols. It is instead a hard, strong, inexorable song about the power of God and the powerlessness of humankind.[7]

In Mary's "yes" to God's invitation, she accepted her part in the historic narrative of communal faith. She accepted her part in the vocation of shalom. In an unprecedented, intimate way, Mary would bear shalom into the world. Her "yes" and Christ's birth inaugurated a new community of peace. Theologically, Mary's "yes" was the next step of God's re-creation. As the first words of John's Gospel indicate, the birth of Jesus was a regenesis. Mary's "yes" was categorically not an individual pietistic event—an internal private faith response to God. To view Mary that way is to read Enlightenment ideas back into Luke's text. Making the conception of Christ into a private event of Marian piety is to capitulate to the worldview that Christian and religious philosopher Charles Taylor calls the "immanent frame," where transcendence is discarded as useless and reality is explained self-referentially.[8]

The culture is caught in an immanent frame. The mechanical world jettisoned a "hierarchy of being" and there was an "atrophy of a sense of God."[9] The transcendent world was rejected in favor of a natural world without mystery. Reality could be explained in reference to itself. There was no need for the individual life to be dependent upon or in relationship with God. Instead, the "buffered human being" was self-sufficient.[10] Even society was able to reveal its own "blueprint" for how things are to "hang together" for the "mutual benefit" of the whole.[11] In the end there would be no need for God or religion. The Church was, all in all, unprepared to speak a living word into this culture shift. In fact, the Church willingly adapted to it and settled into a diaspora relationship with the culture.

Throughout what religious philosopher Robert Bellah classifies as "historic religion" or what we might call "modern Christianity," the Church has operated under the philosophical proposition of the "self," and wrestled with the social implications of this idea. Bellah writes that Christianity attempted to "understand the natural laws of the self's existence, further encouraging personal responsibility, since now we know that humans make their own symbols."[12] This worldview is not something that Mary or her peers would have understood.

We do well to remember that "primitive" and "archaic" religious traditions had no notion of the "self." There was no definition of an individual outside of a community. In the *Magnificat*, Mary made sense of her experience by proclaiming that her pregnancy had made her part of the community of a God who had done mighty acts. She was part of the community who had been raised out of Egypt. And she claimed an active part in God's unfolding narrative of peace.

The difference between Mary's worldview and our own matters in our discussion about our sense of call and vocation. The self-referential immanent frame has disconnected both faithful individual life and communal life from the sphere of public life. Our encounters with God's salvific narrative have become internal private affairs, which is quite the opposite of what God intends when God issues invitations. The modern "self" has partitioned the world in ways Mary could not have imagined, and we cannot see how peculiar our obsession with the "self" is, because it is so fundamental to our worldview. If the conception of Jesus was only a matter for God and Mary, or my experience of grace is simply about God and me, then there is no need for community and it is no longer possible for the arc of shalom to encompass all people—all creation—living together in a single peaceable kingdom.

Mary understood herself as a member of God's community and accepted her role as an active participant in the future trajectory of that community. The narrative that Mary acceded to with her "yes" is the continuing mission of a shalom-making God. God's light and God's mission would reach the ends of the earth through the work of the four Evangelists. The writers of the Gospels understood that Jesus was not just another "suffering servant," but that God in Christ Jesus was undertaking a cosmic work of shalom-making through the power of the Holy Spirit. Mary spoke the comfort that Isaiah earlier proclaimed to the people of God suffering in exile. Lips would be freed so that all the nations would resound in a prophetic acclamation of God's work and mission. The Gospels were hardwired for a universal mission because they interpolated Mary and Jesus into the story that began with Abraham and Sarah. As Paul said to King Agrippa:

> To this day I have had help from God, and so I stand here, testifying to both small and great, saying nothing but what the prophets and Moses said would take place: that the Messiah must suffer, and that, by being the first to rise from the dead, he would proclaim light both to our people and to the Gentiles. (Acts 26:22–23)

God's mission is light to the world, a light of peace that falls on the faithful and the unfaithful alike. The Word conceived in Mary was to be the Prince of Peace—the Prince of Shalom. This child would bring about "endless peace" (Isa. 9:6), which would be a new reign built upon a different righteousness than that of the world. Peace would prevail forever—it is the mission of God and God was zealous for it.

Mary's call story is echoed in the ministry of John the Baptist, who similarly envisioned the mission of God in Christ Jesus as inaugurating this peaceable kingdom. John told the crowds that they must be a different kind of people to join the reign of God. Everyone had to be clothed and fed in this community so that all would have what they needed. The wealthy had to be neighbors to those who had nothing by sharing what they had. The reign of God would inaugurate a just economy where people worked, but did not take advantage of each other's vulnerability, so the poor were not consigned to endless poverty. The reign of God would be a community where even the soldier rejected the policies of the *Pax Romana* (the Peace of Rome) that was built upon threats, false accusations, violence, and death (Luke 3:4–14). The realm of God would be a community with different kinds of members; uniformity would not be a value. People would pursue the vocation of shalom in the midst of everyday life. The reign of God would be a community that lived together differently, bringing judgment upon the practices of nation-states that used power and violence to promote a peace that was no peace.

The unique person of God in Christ Jesus, the perfect revelation of the living Word and eternal Incarnation, was invited to be a blessing of peace in both his baptism and in the story of the Transfiguration. In both events God poured transcendence upon Jesus and revealed to those who were near that he was the Incarnation of God's shalom. For Luke, though, Jesus truly took on the work of shalom during his first visit to the synagogue in Nazareth after a time of traveling.

It was the Sabbath, and Jesus unrolled the scroll to the prophet Isaiah. He began to read. "The Spirit of the Lord is upon me, because he has anointed me to bring good news to the poor. He has sent me to proclaim release to the captives and recovery of sight to the blind, to let the oppressed go free, to proclaim the year of the Lord's favor." He then rolled up the scroll and everyone in the synagogue watched him as he sat back down. Then Jesus said, "Today this scripture has been fulfilled in your hearing" (Luke 4:16–21). Jesus's ministry would mirror what Isaiah foretold when he imagined God's shalom. His community would be for the least and the lost. Jesus would inaugurate a community of release and freedom. He would bring God's blessing of peace into the world so all would know they were beloved of God, for he was the prince of shalom.

As if to live into what has been called "The Nazareth Manifesto," Jesus set about casting a vision for this community.[13] The community was one that was present in the lives of people. The gospel was not simply an idea to be preached, but a life to be lived in and among people. The manifesto of Jesus offered a vision of life lived with the hungry, with the imprisoned, and with the lost and least. His Sermon on the Mount articulated such a vision (Luke 6 and Matt. 5). It is rare that the Gospel writers recorded direct teaching by Jesus. Parables were the primary way he spoke about the kingdom of peace. This direct teaching recorded in Matthew begins with what we have come to call the Beatitudes, because Jesus's words distributed blessings. Again, capturing the narrative of Abraham and Sarah and bringing it forward, people who lived in this new community built around Jesus were a blessing and would be a blessing to the world because they lived *with* the poor. The poor in spirit, those who mourn, the meek, those who deeply long for goodness and faith, those who make mercy happen, the humble, and those in whom there is no guile, all of these people were beloved of God, blessed by God, and they were a blessing to the world (Matt. 5:2–8). These are the people God welcomed into the bosom of blessed Abraham—as in the parable of Lazarus and the rich man (Luke 16:19–31). The least were the first citizens in the reign of peace—a new family outside of the systems of domination.

The second citizens were the peacemakers (Matt. 5:9). The community of shalom was to be filled with peacemakers, and Jesus was committed to growing the number of peacemakers and equipping them for their work. People would know who was a member of the community of shalom because they would live outside of the domination system of powers, authorities, and violence and live into the narrative of waging peace. The peacemakers would join the ranks of God's beloved, and they would be known by the way they lived their lives as children of God. Living as peacemakers, though, would not be peaceful, as Jesus taught later on. Those who were afraid of the authorities and principalities, or who gained from the systems of domination, would not be happy with the peacemakers and would punish, persecute, and martyr them because of the discomfort they felt about the evil that peacemakers revealed in the various edifices of society. For this reason their witness to peace would bring about division between those who were peacemakers and those committed to the status quo of violence and greed. A sharp edge quickly emerged between those who made peace and those who would not join Jesus's community of shalom. This division would not be brought about by the peacemakers, but by those for whom peace only came through violence (Matt. 10:34–39). The keepers of the *Pax Romana* would persecute the peacemakers, who would suffer for righteousness sake. Despite their trials, those who lived in peace, who constituted the community of shalom, would participate in God's reign in this world and the next. Those who were reviled and persecuted, who had all kinds of evil muttered against them because of their witness to God's peace and their participation in the great narrative arc of God, would join the ranks of Abraham, Sarah, Moses, Esther, Isaiah, and Jonah (Matt. 5:10–11).

We need to read the Beatitudes as a call to the members of the new community. They were the marching orders. Jesus's voice echoed over the hillside, declaring that his disciples were to bless the world like the patriarchs, matriarchs, judges, and prophets before them. They were to be salt. They were to be light. Salt and light were images often used for the religious elite. Jesus appropriated the images and offered them to the new members of the community. It would not be a new religion or a renewal of an old religion. It was no religion at all. Like the Sinai prophets before him, Jesus spoke out against the religion of the day. He called into existence a community of mutuality that did not use religious hierarchy to oppress, or create a religious economy that enriched the privileged. Jesus's community would be people who served God with no religious domination. It was a higher way of living together (Matt. 5:11–21).

Much of religion is about forcing others to become something they are not. God's desire in sending us out into the world to serve, on the other hand, is about enabling us to become something we *are*: members of the body of Christ, a community that knows and extends God's shalom to the world. *This* community will create relationships of peace. The human way of practicing religion manufactures systems of violence and oppression. Jesus's community has a higher rule of peacemaking. It is concerned with restoring broken relationships and making peace among neighbors, which means all people (Matt. 5:21–26). Women are not objects to be coveted or property with no self-determination. Women and men will live together in healthy relationships (Matt. 5:26–32).

Finally, Jesus called his disciples to be a community of honesty. They were invited to speak truthfully and not engage in sophistry—the use words to gain power (Matt. 5:33–37). They were invited to be salt and light by becoming peacemakers who joyfully sacrificed themselves for each other. Moreover, they were called to give their lives for their enemies as well as their friends (Matt. 5:38–48; John 15:9–17).

The Word of God spoke God's mission of shalom into existence as creation itself was birthed. Jesus, the Word made flesh, now articulates these blessings with ever more clarity in the Beatitudes. Jesus said with clarity that God's intention was for the community of shalom to witness against the systems of domination by reversing them.[14] Theologian Walter Wink calls this inauguration a "domination free order."[15] The peacemaking community was an alternative to communities based upon sibling rivalry, the repeated (mimetic) desire for improvement of one's own state over and against our brother or sister, as in the story of Cain and Abel. The peacemaking community was an alternative to communities that lived by the law of vengeance, where women are property, violence against other tribes was sanctioned, and religion was linked with the powers of the nation-state. The peacemaking community rejected wealth as a driver of connection and source of power, thereby setting aside practices of economic oppression, so that all were fed and had what they needed for shelter, clothing, care, and sustenance. The Jesus movement, if it was to be a movement at all, had to loose the economy of the community of shalom from elements of violence. In Matthew 6:19–34, Jesus replaced a dark violent vision of community with trust in God and pursuit of life in God's new order.[16] Socially, politically, religiously, economically, Jesus subverted the domination system and the spirit that drives it.

The peaceable kingdom is deeply connected to the call stories and vocation of Israel covered in the prior chapter. The reign of peace is less concerned with order and control and more concerned with enabling all of us to play our part in the narrative arc of God's love. Seeing the world through the lens of shalom cannot be undone, though it can be rejected in favor of a personal *Pax Romana* that perpetuates economic and social violence for the sake of individual or tribal peace. There are plenty of authority figures who pretend that "peace" in the world can be purchased by violence, but that is a complete rejection of Christ's reign of shalom, which is purchased by loving enemies and laying down swords. The peace of God is purchased by Christ's victimhood and not by God's own violence. God's story of peace is rooted like a cedar of Lebanon in the world by the suffering God-man, and not by a faithful war led by disciples. When Peter dared to raise a sword to protect the Savior, Jesus healed the man wounded by his blade and told Peter the kingdom of peace could not be saved by violence (John 18:10–12).

Christ chose to honor his place in this narrative of peace. Christ, whose equality with God was already established, bridged the gap between heaven and earth between God and humanity (Phil. 2:5–11). Christ's invitation, preaching, and his sacrificial death inaugurated a peace that passes all understanding, giving us the possibility for peace in our own lives (Phil. 4:7). Through our own participation in God's great gift of death and then resurrection, we find peace. We find peace with ourselves, with others, our enemies, and with the God who remains so different from us.[17] Jesus puts flesh on this vision of the divine community. Jesus calls us to go. We are God's messengers of this kingdom of peace. Isaiah prophesies:

> The wolf shall live with the lamb, the leopard shall lie down with the kid, the calf and the lion and the fatling together, and a little child shall lead them. The cow and the bear shall graze, their young shall lie down together; and the lion shall eat straw like the ox. The nursing child shall play over the hole of the asp, and the weaned child shall put its hand on the adder's den. They will not hurt or destroy on all

my holy mountain; for the earth will be full of the knowledge of the
LORD as the waters cover the sea. (Isa. 11:6–9)

This kind of shalom is possible because God in Christ Jesus becomes a
victim. There is no victory without victimization by the powers that be.
Jesus's final laying of the foundation stone of the peaceable kingdom was
in his willingness to die for the righteous and the unrighteous alike, and
to be raised for the righteous and unrighteous alike (Matt. 5:45). This is
much more than the notion that life is sacred. What is particularly unique
and separates Christianity from religion is that Christ gives himself over
for the sake of the criminals, enemies, hatemongers, violence makers, and
victimizers too. As Christians who follow this Christ, we not only give
ourselves over to the other, but we are also responsible for the sacredness
of life that belongs to our neighbor and enemy alike. To divide the world
into groups of people whose lives are expendable and those whose lives
are sacred is to create communal action contrary to the will and actions of
God in Christ Jesus. God imagines a different kind of faith community
altogether. In the great tradition of the Sinai prophets over and against a
temple-centric faith engaged in nation-building, Jesus inaugurated a community with organizing grounded in the historic community of Abraham
and Sarah, and in the Creation narrative itself. While creation was brought
forth out of nothing (*ex nihilo*), the shalom community arouses the memory of Edenic fellowship among its members. The memory of Eden is the
icon of the Incarnation—a longing for such harmony is found in each
human being by their very nature as a creature of God.

Jesus was killed by humanity as a reenactment of ancient religious
sacrifice. He participated totally in the mimetic sacrifice. If that were the
end of it, then we would be invested in just another community with a
scapegoat theology that repeated the violence of mythic gods. But God
took our violence and broke it open. Jesus was raised from the dead by
God and in so doing, Girard says, God "refutes the whole principle of violence and sacrifice. God is revealed as the 'arch-scapegoat,' the completely
innocent one who dies in order to give life. And his way of giving life is to
overthrow the religion of scapegoating and sacrifice—which is the essence

of myth." The Old Testament narrative reveals God to be the maker of shalom that undoes the endless sibling rivalries and repeated sacrifices that bend humankind toward vengeance. The story of Jesus lines up with the stories of Cain and Abel, Joseph, Job, and the Psalms, as well as the experience of Moses and the Israelites in Egypt. The story of the people of shalom is a story that reverses all scapegoat typologies. Christ is innocent and reveals the violence and scapegoating of the world. Only in the shalom community's innocence can people strive for peace and reveal the violence that dominates every age.[18]

God in Christ Jesus, the incarnation made flesh in history, enables an anthropological reading of the scripture that reverses human violence and reveals the community of peace. We begin to understand that inside our shared monstrosity, there is a fragment of humanity in perfect communion with God. Wink says we are "fleetingly human, brokenly human."[19] We are created in the very image of the Incarnation: "Only God is human, and we are made in God's image and likeness—which is to say, we are capable of becoming human."[20] Jesus the Prince of Peace helps us glimpse our true humanity by revealing a capacity for peace-building that has been deep within us since our creation.

Jesus turns our inherited notions about God upside down. We discover that we have been a part of religious systems of domination. We believed that God requires Jesus's death, making God a mythic monster. We believed that we should be grateful for this sacrifice because of our monstrous flesh. We attended church and gave generously in order to undo our fleshly sin, make recompense for our evil, and gain eternal life. The medieval church innovated a theory of atonement that remains popular today. This theology built cathedrals and lined the purses of many clerics. However, substitutionary atonement theory does not line up with the story of the sacrifice of Isaac, where God made clear that no human sacrifices were required. It does not line up with the idea that humans are modeled on the eternal Incarnation. Moreover, this theory of the atonement sanctions the commission of violence against others in many varying and inhumane forms for the sake of peace. By contrast, the gospel of peace reveals God as a victim of violence, and as a human worth saving. This gospel reveals that we are connected to the Incarnation itself, in our innermost parts. Living and following Jesus is about embracing the Incarnation and rejecting the old mimetic tendencies that inevitably find their way back into religion—even Christianity. By the grace of God, the Incarnation is our hope and our potential. The world is truly turned upside down by the resurrection of God in Christ Jesus.

God is interested in a continuing narrative of peace making and community building. Mary says "Yes" to this work and makes the uniqueness of God in Christ Jesus possible. Jesus himself, being found in human form, does not inaugurate an institutional church but rather the community of shalom that has been part of the story since the foundations of creation were set. Christ and his body are the actual icon of our realized humanness. His body is also the image of the community at work. Where he goes, what he does, who he meets, and what he says are ways the community of shalom works in the world around us. If the Church is to be Christ's body in the world, then it must engage in the work of shalom. It must make new communities of shalom. It must resist powers, authorities, and the violence they beget in this world. Therefore, any vocations emanating from the Church must bring about Christ's shalom community—a blessed community of peace for the sake of the world.

CHAPTER THREE

Disciples of Peace

I love to think of them at dawn
Beneath the frail pink sky,
Casting their nets in Galilee
And fish-hawks circling by.
Casting their nets in Galilee
Just off the hills of brown
Such happy, simple fisherfolk
Before the Lord came down.

—William Alexander Percy[1]

The Gospels differ in their account of how Jesus and his disciples begin their ministry. Nonetheless, a common pattern emerges: Jesus's ministry begins after his baptism and his journey in the wilderness, as John the Baptist is fading away. Jesus boldly renounces worldly power and violence during his conflict with the devil in the desert. This powerful renunciation foreshadows the choices Jesus makes throughout his ministry: the community he founds, and the reign he reinvigorates will demonstrate God's intentions. Through Jesus, God creates an intentional community of shalom.

The first two disciples that Jesus brought into this community were two brothers, Simon (who is Peter) and Andrew. Jesus came across them as he walked by the Sea of Galilee. They were fishing from the shore. Jesus invited them to follow (Mark 1:16–18; Matt. 4:18–19). They dropped their nets and followed immediately. A little further along, they picked up James and John—the sons of Zebedee (Mark 1:19–20; Matt. 4:19–22). John's Gospel tells us that Andrew brought Peter to Jesus after John the Baptist pointed him out. Jesus said to Andrew, "Come and see" (John 1:35–42). The disciples took Jesus's invitation because they believed that he had inherited the mantle of John the Baptist. Jesus was the one about whom John had been preaching. John's Gospel continues with Philip in Galilee. Philip and his brother Nathanael came to Jesus. Jesus is proclaimed as the one "about whom Moses in the law and also the prophets wrote" (John 1:43–51). Significantly, Nathanael believed that Jesus was to be the king of Israel. Jesus flatly rejected the revolution Nathanael implied. Jesus's kingdom is to be a reign of peace, and not borne from the world of violence (John 1:10; John 14:17). As the disciples came and saw, they discovered that they too were called to inaugurate a reign of peace and reject the world of violence (John 15:18; 17:20–26).

The first disciples Jesus encountered beside the Sea of Galilee were invited to be "fishers of people." This is not a general invitation to follow. It is not a mere pun. The Church's unconscious habit of reading scripture as legitimating text for a vast institution has made these call stories about bringing people to Jesus and church growth. The call stories represent how church members should bring other people to church where they can meet Jesus. Within the narrative arc of the shalom community, these stories have a different meaning.

"Fishers of people" create the shalom community itself. By calling his disciples to become fishers of men, Jesus harkened back to the holy narrative of the Old Testament and the patriarchs and matriarchs God called to make a community for all people.[2] The first mention of this metaphor in the narrative of God is found in the prophecy of Jeremiah:

> I am now sending for many fishermen, says the LORD, and they shall catch them; and afterward I will send for many hunters, and they shall hunt them from every mountain and every hill, and out of the clefts of the rocks. (Jer. 16:16)

The people of Israel had forgotten their call to build a community of sha-lom. Jeremiah was reminding them that they were to be a community of blessing to the world. They were to take care of the poor and the least and the lost. The blood of the innocent poor were on Israel's hands (Jer. 2:35). Through Jeremiah, God said that the leaders of God's people had been poor shepherds, scattering the people when they were supposed to gather them (Jer. 23:1–6). God pledged to overturn Israel because it had forgot-ten itself and its God (Jer. 18:15; 30:14). God intended to gather God's people anew, and frustrate those who preyed on the poor. The image of "fishing for people" returned in the prophesies of Amos (4:2). Through the prophet Amos, God declared that those who forget the needy and live upon their backs would be taken away by fishhooks. And again in Habakkuk (1:13–16), God would catch the people up in God's dragnet. Ezekiel prophesied that the people were the fish and would be gathered in (29:3b–4).

Jesus used the image of fishing for people to convey that his mission was in line with God's mission of ancient days. Using the Old Testament and language of Palestine, Jesus declared his intention to gather God's people into a new reign of peace (Matt. 23:37–39). This gathering included the rich and the poor, the found and the lost. All people would be gathered into a community of peace; exploitation, injustice, and violence of any sort were unknown. In this community, neither the poor nor the rich would become scapegoats. God's people would be gathered in like fish caught in a dragnet. Jesus's message was consistent with the scriptural narrative from Abraham and Sarah to Mary. So when Jesus called these fishermen from the Sea of Galilee, Jesus invited them to be part of a different community doing a different kind of work. Their way in life was to be different from the world of violence that surrounded them. They were joining Jesus in his work of shalom. Remember, the reign of God was near. The captives were to be released, the blind to receive sight, and the oppressed to be unbound. God's blessing was proclaimed, all were to be gathered in, and a new order of living was to be established (Luke 4:16–19).

Let us pause here and speak of the word *vocation* because Jesus was definitely not inviting these fishermen into a church job or an engaging hobby, which is how many of us understand vocation in the Church today. If we are not careful, our ingrained expectation of a professional class of clergy will quickly sabotage our ability to understand the ministry of Jesus and the disciples. Our bias builds churchy furniture into this story where there is none. We put our church goggles on and read the idea that the disciples called on that seashore were the first priests of the church back into the scripture. They used to make money as fishermen, then they made their money as ministers (Luke 10:4–11). This was not the case.

The root of the word *vocation* is the word *voice*. A related term is *vocāre*, which means "call"—to be "called was to be invited to do this or that."[3] The meaning of vocation, as we have been using it, is a call to "go" on God's behalf. Vocation is about being invited to go be the voice of God. This is not a professional obligation, but rather a dynamic partnership of humans with God that has persisted from the very beginning. Adam and Eve worked with God in the caretaking of the Garden and creation. God walked with them in the evening to survey the work they were doing together. Humans have always been invited to join God and to "till it and keep it" (Gen. 2:15). We are possessed by God's invitation to speak and be a blessing to the world. We are occupied with undoing the violence of the world by ending the cycles of sibling rivalry. Humans are uniquely suitable to this vocation.

Martin Luther and John Calvin regularly thought of vocation as a community at work, though they were not the first.[4] The Middle Ages imbued vocation with an expectation of special training or craft skill. The guilds promoted this idea of vocation, and bound up the practice of the professions in religious ritual.[5] Only after the sixteenth century was the term *vocation* regularly used to describe the priesthood. Modern Christians and humanist philosophers strained the sacred meanings out of the idea of vocation over time, and eventually participation in the church became an optional avocation, unless you were part of the clerical hierarchy, and then church work was your vocation—your professional work. Such a partitioning between religious obligation and professional obligation is foreign to the scriptures. The disciples were called into the community of God's peace. They were invited to be God's voice and to cooperate with Jesus in making a different community that rejected violence.

Let us return to the disciples on the shore of the Sea of Galilee. Luke's Gospel tells the story of the calling of the first disciples as a fishing miracle. Jesus came by and taught the people using the boat as a platform. He then invited the disciples to cast out into the sea and to put out their nets. The fishermen doubted, as they had been fishing all night with nothing to show for their efforts. They did as Jesus said and a great multitude of fish was brought aboard. Luke tells us that their nets were breaking. They called other boats to come and help. Peter immediately told Jesus he was not worthy to follow. Jesus told Peter, James, and John to join him and he would teach them to fish for people (Luke 5:1–11). At the end of John's Gospel there is a companion story, where Jesus appeared on the seashore and called out to his followers who had gone fishing, ordering them to cast their net on the others side of the boat. Again, they did so, and multitudes of fish were brought in. They joined Jesus for breakfast and he revealed himself as the risen Christ on the shore in the breaking of the bread. Jesus then invited them to be leaders in the new community of shalom. He said, "Follow me" (John 21:1–19). These two miracles gesture toward the work of fishing for people, and demonstrate that the reign of God is a community of shalom.

In the Gospel of Matthew, chapter thirteen, Jesus returned to fishing images when he said, "The kingdom of heaven is like a net that was thrown into the sea and caught fish of every kind" (v. 47). This parable was the last among a long series about the kingdom of peace. Robert Farrar Capon uses this parable to speak eschatologically about the kingdom to come at the end of the age. I think Jesus was also speaking of the reign that is at hand in this world. So while I concur with Capon's interpretation,[6] I want to broaden it to fit into a wider discussion of the disciples' work as peace builders, because followers of Jesus are doing work in this world that will remain at the end of the age. Jesus used the dragnet as a metaphor for this peace-making enterprise. The community the disciples build was to be universal and catholic—everyone was included.

Dragnets gather in everything because they dredge the sea floor. They capture wood and plants as well as fish. They capture inedible fish as well as edible fish. The community of peace that Jesus inaugurated in this world has the same characteristic of indiscriminateness. God is making a community that connects, or net-works, all kinds of people. While we normally think of this kingdom-net only containing fish, and good fish at that, it truly contains everything: the weeds, the detritus of dysfunctional relationships and human brokenness, the debris of daily life lived in service to the masters of economies and political powermongers. The community of shalom, our dragnet, "touches everything in the world: not just souls, but bodies, and not just people, but all things, animal, vegetable, and mineral."[7] God in Christ Jesus is in this very world gathering into the community of shalom the whole of creation. As God in Christ was lifted up on the cross, the great crossroads of community was bridged—heaven with earth, humanity with God. All was drawn to God's self (John 12:32). As the book of Revelation indicates, all of creation is drawn to God in Christ—not just people.

The disciples were called to participate in the transfiguration of the world, which is partly why they were led down from the mountainside after Jesus's transfiguration. They were to be the transfigured Christ in the world. The work of transfiguring creation only happens down in the village where demons are cast out and people are healed (Matt. 17:1–27). The mystery of the community of shalom is that it includes God and people and must also include the whole of creation. Secular moderns, imprisoned as we are in our immanent frame, want to differentiate between what is worth capturing in the net and what is not, but no such distinction is made in the parables of the kingdom in the Gospels.[8] The dragnet rejects nothing in the sea; it encompasses all things. The only people missing from God's dragnet when it is hauled ashore will be those who carve themselves out of the net with their own sickle of judgment. This is what the scriptures imply when they say that the sickle will soon enough come for those who refuse the community of peace and instead choose power, abuse of the poor by neglect, and do violence to others and creation (Matt. 25:31–46; Rev. 14). The sickle comes for those who cannot live with the least, the lost, and the unclean. They have spent their whole life being different from those "other" people. They hold too much judgment in their heart, keeping track of the negative marks against others. It is difficult for people who routinely use their power and authority to keep others down to accept that God has invited everyone into the reign of peace. I pray that it will be very difficult indeed to resist God's grace, to deny God's sacrifice is enough even for my enemy, and to reject God's love when I come face-to-face with God's eternal peace.[9]

The story of scripture also tells us that the separation of judgment will not take place before the transfiguration at the end of the age. There is always time. In this hope we live and work and have our being. Between now and the end of time, the disciples of Jesus can reject nothing, for the dragnet rejects nothing, and the community of peace has no "business setting itself up in the judging business. And, neither, a fortiori, does the church."[10] The disciples are to follow Jesus and learn from him, as participants in the great narrative of God's shalom. We are to learn how this new dragnet of community is to hold all kinds of people. This is how the band of Jesus followers become a "sacrament," the continuing body of Christ in the world. We will have to "avoid the temptation to act like a sport fishermen who is interested only in speckled trout and hand-tied flies," says Capon.[11] Disciples are called to be the worst kind of fishers. The only thing we are to discard is the temptation to reject the mess of creation and humanity. Our community of shalom in this world participates in the reign of God at the end of the age if it remains in relationship with all the "old boots, bottles, and beer cans" that a truly random dredging of humanity must be. The Church will be transfigured to the extent that it is one and the same with the mess it intends to drag in.[12]

To point out how important this work is, Luke follows the call story of the disciples with an encounter with a leper. Lepers were shunned from the religious community of the day. Their illness made intimacy and belonging impossible. Lepers were seen as sinful and unworthy of community membership, but Jesus restored one such leper back to the community by engagement with the God of creation. God's Living Word made the leper whole, rejecting the status quo. God in Christ Jesus engaged someone who was not to be engaged (Luke 5:12–16). Moreover, Jesus tied his healing of the leper into the story of Moses.

After the call story in Mark, Jesus went to the home of Peter, where they found his mother-in-law on death's door. Jesus brought the dragnet of peace into Peter's home, and there restored the woman into community (Mark 1:29–31).

In Matthew's version of the call story, there is a fight between Jesus and the religious powers that be. They were concerned about Jesus's congregating with sinners. Jesus's next action was to call a sinner to participate in the community of shalom, a tax collector named Levi (Matt. 9:9). Levi participated in the systemic oppression of the poor by supporting the *Pax Romana* and the religious powers in league with Rome. He participated in a system of "peace" enforced by religious and political violence. Levi collected the seven layers of taxes that oppressed the people while lining the purses of the powerful. Of course he added some cost into the mix for his own trouble, as was the tradition for tax collectors. Jesus invited this sinner, this corrupt player in the systems of violence and oppression, to follow and to join a different community—the community of God's shalom. Levi received the call and left his table (Matt. 9:9). Jesus then took Levi with him into a home. Again, Jesus placed the new community of shalom within a home and at a table. Here Levi, one of the undesirables, an inedible fish, joined Jesus and other tax collectors and sinners and they ate together (Matt. 9:10). Jesus responded to the critics, explaining that the community of shalom was like the dragnet, made up of many who the religious and the political establishment saw as unfit. The community of shalom was not populated with worthy heroes resplendent in glory. It was composed of unworthy and unlikely human beings who had renounced systems of violence out of a hunger for peace. They had rejected sibling rivalry. They were random contents of the dragnet—the good fish and bad.

The only place in the Near East where such a heterogeneous community could be assembled was in the Galilee, Nazareth, and Capernaum—places outside of orbit of Jerusalem. Jesus's work was only possible at the margins of society, because that was where the mixture of misfits was to be found. In the Gospels the kingdom of peace always took root in the wilderness—out in the countryside. As the reign of peace began to take root, it immediately came into conflict with the powers of state and religion. Its very existence challenged the accepted norms of social behavior that protected the powerful. Transgressing these norms brought violence. So to accept the call to speak the voice of shalom brought the violence of the systems of oppression down upon the follower of Jesus. Mark's Gospel provides an example. From the beginning Jesus ate with sinners, challenging accepted religious and social boundaries (Mark 2:15). Jesus challenged religious purity codes by being in contact with lepers (Mark 1:41). He gave food to the hungry (Mark 2:23). All of this created conflict with the authorities (Mark 1:22; 1:43; 2:6; and 2:15). By the time Jesus and his disciples have traveled for three years building their community of peace, the Roman political machinery, the Jewish religious hierarchy, and the most revered clerical powers decided that violence was the only solution to the threat that Jesus's community posed to their power and they plotted to kill him (Mark 3:1–6).

The reign of peace demands a transfiguration of the community and portends radical change for the institutions that enforce order. Jesus's own experience demonstrates that building the kingdom of shalom requires direct confrontation with the powers of this world. In Mark's Gospel, Jesus took on the powers of religion that preyed on humanity and in the next moment he took on the powers of the state which did the same. Jesus wanted to show all who followed him what was in store for them. New Testament scholar and activist Ched Myers writes, "Thus at the heart of Mark's Gospel is the assertion that the messianic vocation—and our discipleship as well—is defined by redemptive suffering, not triumph."[13]

Beyond this kind of "show and tell," Jesus provided very little "formation" for "laypeople"—here called disciples. There was no Inquirers 101 class. They followed Jesus and Jesus revealed how the reign of shalom was enacted. This was done traveling here and there. They remained in the countryside and stayed in people's homes. Jesus visited and touched and ate with people who were outside of the boundaries of his society. He visited with Samaritans, lepers, women, tax collectors, and the poor. But just when we think we have Jesus figured out and are ready to declare that he was on the side of the outcast, he also ate with the rich, the religious leaders, and the like. They even came to visit him at night (John 3:2).

Jesus tended not to enter into conversations with an agenda, allowing his purposes to reveal themselves in a natural way. Jesus was always honest about the reign of peace and how it caught people. He did not shy away from difficult conversations, and he appeared, as in the case of the rich young man, to begin every encounter with a sense of love for the other. The disciples followed along, and we assume they were watching and learning. They asked questions from time to time. Rarely did Jesus pull them aside and talk with them specifically.

A disciple is "one who follows." The church in recent years has fallen in love with the words *disciple* and *discipleship*. This is natural because the Church as an institution likes to have followers; but followers do not remain passive in the community of shalom. Every disciple becomes an apostle. An apostle is "one who goes." The institutional Church reserves the term *apostle* for those ordained as bishops. As much as I, a bishop, would like this to be true, it is not. In the scripture, all of the disciples became apostles because everyone who followed Jesus was meant to "go." The apostles were part of the narrative arc of shalom that reached back to Abraham and Sarah. Those who were called into the shalom community went in God's name, spoke with God's voice, blessed the people they came into contact with, and were a blessing to the world. Jesus called the group together, gave them a blessing, and told them to go out and do what he had been doing. They were to cast out demons, unbind people, cure disease, heal people, and announce the kingdom of peace.

Jesus told his apostles to travel light: no staff, bag, bread, money—not even extra clothes. When they got to a house, if they were invited, stay (Matt. 26:6). If they were not welcomed, pass through (Luke 4:28–30). They went to do the same work that Jesus did, in the same manner that Jesus did. Their ministry of peace was so renowned that people thought John the Baptist had been raised from the dead, Elijah had returned, or the ancient prophets had been raised because the apostles were performing great acts of shalom as the great prophets had done in their day (Luke 9:7–9). In the people's eyes, the apostles' ministry of community-making was linked to the ancient narrative of peace-making that Israel remembered from the scriptures. The apostles finally returned and told all that they had done and what they saw and they were astounded (Luke 9:10–11). People began to surround the apostles because their needs were great. The community of shalom grew. Together, the apostles fed them and more followed.

We are told that the community was growing and that there were other disciples: other followers called to be the voice of God's peace to the world. So Jesus turned them into apostles as well. Jesus appointed, called, and invited seventy more (Luke 10:1). He sent them in pairs to go to every town and every place. Jesus told them the world needed them. The world needed the blessing of their growing community of peace. Jesus said, "The harvest is plentiful, but the laborers are few; therefore ask the Lord of the harvest to send out laborers into his harvest" (Luke 10:2). He told them, as he told the smaller group of apostles privately, that when the kingdom of peace comes into contact with the world, it would be costly. He told them it would be a struggle. It had always been a struggle. It was a struggle for their faith ancestors. They would learn as they went. He gave these seventy, these thirty-five mission pairings, the same instruction he gave the Twelve: travel light (Luke 10:3–4). Jesus also said, "Whatever house you enter, first say, 'Peace to this house!' And if anyone is there who shares in peace, your peace will rest on that person; but if not, it will return to you" (Luke 10:5–6). He told them to announce that the community they were making was one of God's peace and that it was near to all who wished to be a part of it. They were to do the mighty works of God by feeding people, curing the sick, and casting out demons (Luke 10:10–11). Jesus also told them that they were to depend on their hosts for shelter, food, and whatever else they needed. They deserve to be paid (Luke 10:7–9). They were to go in the name of God to be a blessing, and they were to speak a word of shalom for God. Jesus said, "Whoever listens to you listens to me, and whoever rejects you rejects me, and whoever rejects me rejects the one who sent me" (Luke 10:16). They went as apostles, and returned saying, "Lord, in your name even the demons submit to us!" Jesus then said to them, "I watched Satan fall from heaven like a flash of lightning" (Luke 10:17–18).

God in Christ Jesus did not invite a professional class of people to "go" and make real the reign of peace in the world. Jesus clearly called a lot of people, gave them little instruction, and sent them out to make the kingdom of peace real. There was no formal training. There was no elongated process of discernment. There was no three-year training course for the baptized or the clergy. There was God's invitation to go, a willingness to accept the invitation and become apostles, and a shared understanding that they were to speak a word of peace to all those they met. There was no guarantee other than God's promise of presence in the work of making peace. In this way, the kingdom of shalom would continue its work of taking root in the lives of humans. And, finally, there was the reality that it would be costly. Jesus was not starting a new sedentary mission. Over and over again those who had some sense of stability were called out and sent in God's name on a difficult mission they were not prepared for, and they invited others into the vocation of tending creation in partnership with God.

Though they understood that the community of shalom existed in the world, they were to be different from the world. Yes, there were economics involved. Judas himself was the purse bearer responsible for the finances of the community and sharing what they had with the poor (John 13:29). Yes, they were to have food and shelter and to even be paid. And there would also be sacrifice. Living into the community of shalom meant living into the way of the Cross. They would be required to rethink how community lived and worked together in the world. There would be debate about the wealth of the community and how it was used. There would be conversations about how people treated one another and how to take care of each other. Ensuring that everyone is cared for and fed within the community of shalom would be a key ingredient to the difficult task of being a community of God's peace. But there would also be the oppression of violence that would threaten the community because of its stand and its witness.

We have already talked above about the cost of this following. Enduring violence as a peaceful apostle of God is very much part of this vocation for each of us individually and for the Church as a whole. Apostleship is never a mantle we shoulder alone; we share it as part of the community of shalom. The problem for such a community is that, like Peter on the roadside near Caesarea Philippi, we constantly wish to see Jesus as a messiah of earthly power (Mark 8:27–30). Those who follow Jesus struggle against the notion that the reign of peace is a more benevolent reign of power. The followers of Jesus argued about where they would sit at the eschatological banquet (Mark 10:37) and even at the Last Supper (Luke 22:27–30). Even though they had chosen to follow Jesus and go out into the world to further the reign of peace, they struggled to renounce the age-old script of power and violence. Even liberation theologians fall prey to Peter's mistake.[14] The myth of redemptive violence that René Girard spoke about so often is always knocking on the door. But, against all human wisdom, the Christ and his followers make a community of peace by rejecting violence and instead in favor of Christ's love and his victimhood. The ancient sibling rivalries that animate our institutions of violence can only be challenged by a community of people willing to serve as peacemakers. Christ's victory is secured by those who lay down both their weapons and their lives for the sake of shalom.

Ched Myers writes, "Jesus's first call to discipleship invited people to 'leave' their places in the prevailing social and economic order, and to 'follow' him in reclaiming the Jubilary vision and God's sovereignty. A second call now articulates the political consequences of that practice ([Mark] 8:34)."[15] The work of the community of peace is to go and speak for God. Doing so means declaring peace in a world of violence, and such a declaration will sometimes mean that the members of Christ's community of peace will lose their lives. The community of shalom is a community that is willing to lose. This is most clearly articulated in the three sayings of Jesus about "the way." Jesus said, "For those who want to save their life will lose it" (Mark 8:35); "Whoever wants to be first must be last of all and servant of all" (Mark 9:35); and, "whoever wishes to become great among you must be your servant" (Mark 10:43). The victory of the cross is no worldly victory; it is complete loss and victimhood. The vocation of the Church is to accept this loss and victimhood as "our way." When it looks like the powers and authorities have won, Christians proclaim that "Jesus's nonviolent power has actually begun to unravel their rule of domination."[16] As Paul wrote in his letter to the Colossians, "He disarmed the rulers and authorities and made a public example of them, triumphing over them in it" (2:15). The community of shalom will continue as many apostles take up their own understanding of this mission and walk out into Easter morning.

CHAPTER FOUR

A Gospel of Peace Takes Root

The Christian, however, must bear the burden of a brother. He must suffer and endure the brother. It is only when he is a burden that another person is really a brother and not merely an object to be manipulated. The burden of men was so heavy for God Himself that He had to endure the Cross. God verily bore the burden of men[sic] in the body of Jesus Christ. But He bore them as a mother carries her child, as a shepherd enfolds the lost lamb that has been found. God took men upon Himself and they weighted Him to the ground, but God remained with them and they with God. In bearing with men God maintained fellowship with them. It was the law of Christ that was fulfilled in the Cross. And Christians must share in this law.

—Dietrich Bonhoeffer[1]

The community of shalom is, by definition, a diversity of people living together. The community of shalom establishes an ethic of peace that incarnates the body of Christ by going out into the world as the voice of God and rejecting the violence of the world. The polity of the community of shalom differs from the structures and powers of the world and stands as a sign of Christ's judgment against those structures and powers by virtue of how different it is. The community of shalom embraces the sacrificial giving of self for the other. This dynamic of self-sacrifice between the community and those outside of it is characteristic of Jesus and was also characteristic of the first communities created by the apostles of shalom as they ventured into the wider world after the Resurrection.

These early churches were ambivalent to the social station and reputation of individual members because the community of shalom welcomed all: the rich, the poor, the prisoner, the jailer, the hungry, sick, and the lost. Jesus spent time with the good, the bad, and the ugly. William Stringfellow wrote that he believed himself to be acceptable in the sight of grace because Jesus spent time with "whores and tax collectors, the blind and the idiotic, lepers and insurrectionists, the poor and those possessed by demons."[2] The kingdom of peace is indiscriminate in its mission. God's expansive invitation is the condition for acceptance, not the random birth lottery of prestige. The ministry of apostleship grows out of true love for outsiders.[3]

The work of an apostle, from the first ones sent out by Jesus to anyone aligned with the reign of peace, is to be God's loving word to every part of the world. Echoing the Word, they are sent out to confront the powers and principalities by rejecting state violence and revolutionary violence, and, instead, putting on the armor of peace (Eph. 6:15). As in the book of Acts, apostles must maintain God's "redemptive vigilance" over their new communities.[4] To put things simply, today's Church must serve the world in Christ's name if it intends to mirror the community of shalom that Jesus first imagined. The apostolic ethic of service must be renewed. When institutional survival is our chief concern, violence infects the very gospel created to contain it. The church of Acts wasted no time pontificating about growth or obsessing over the health of the institution. Instead, the church of Acts put its energy into going, sharing, caring, and serving in peace.

The apostles of the church of Acts were not professionals. They were not climbing a career ladder. When apostleship becomes a career, we turn the Church into a principality or a power—an infection of violence that begins in the subtlest, most innocent of ways. Institutionalizing apostleship is a faithless means of ensuring survival. Stringfellow warns that institutions shape leaders more often than leaders shape institutions. In an institutionalized Church, authentic apostleship and the impulse for mission are the first casualties.[5] For the Church to truly undertake its vocation, it must produce disciples whose apostleship looks like Jesus's own, as opposed to bureaucratic paper pushing. The Church must look outside of itself for means of reform. It must use the tools of vision and mission to reconnect with the narrative arc of the community of peace. While we must accept that the Church *is* a principality, we must also read Acts so that we can reform it in every way possible, in hope that it may become a most "exemplary principality."[6]

The key to such a new life within a reformed, diverse community of shalom is a determined willingness to gather different kinds of people together. Jesus gathered people of every kind throughout his ministry; so too did the Acts church, as illustrated throughout the book of Acts. Sometimes the foreigner who desires to join the community introduces a note of diversity. The Holy Spirit bid Philip to join a eunuch on the roadside. There the eunuch, a person without citizenship or value in society, asked Philip to explain the gospel and baptize him so he could participate in a community that rejected the power of violence (Acts 8:26–40). Likewise, the conversion of the Roman centurion by Peter reveals that the community of peace can accept a warrior. Peter was sent to him, and Peter had to deal with the centurion's murderous vocation, and his nonkosher diet. Acts shows that the early Church was often challenged by its own diversity. Similar to the decision to lay aside the necessity of circumcision, the community laid aside the food codes of the Jewish law for the sake of its mission. As a result, a soldier of the hated Roman Empire and his household that did not keep kosher were numbered among the community of shalom (Acts 10:1–48). Paul had a vision to go to Macedonia. Once there, he was faced with the task of converting a rich woman who dealt in purple: Lydia. She freely received the gospel message, was baptized, and gave her home to be used for the mission (Acts 16:6–15).[7]

What happened in all of these stories was a Spirit-led reorganization of the communal cognitive map. From the day of Pentecost (Acts 2:5–11) onward, Jesus's shalom community came into repeated contact with people outside of the accepted circle of faith centered in Jerusalem and outside the norms of the religion practiced there. Jesus broke these norms open, but in Acts we see the process accelerated as the apostles went out to all parts of the known world. Such porous boundaries were essential to the shalom community's mission. The narrative arc of scripture is not that Abraham and Sarah and their descendants were sent to Jerusalem, but that they and all who came after them would bless the whole world. Jesus's movement of peace adapted to the contexts it found in the mission field. A diversity of people gathered into the community of shalom, *and* at the same time, that same diversity of people challenged the norms that boundaried that community, requiring the Church to adapt for the sake of peace.

The apostolic Church's means of gathering itself has a few qualities worthy of our attention. The Church gathered to baptize, lay hands on each other, tell the sacred story, and eat a common meal of thanksgiving. Baptism was a means of becoming a recognized member (Acts 2:41). As soon as Paul had his conversion experience, he was baptized and began to do the work of the gospel (Acts 9:18). We know that the laying on of hands to invite the Holy Spirit to come down upon the Church was important (Acts 8:14–15).[8] The combination of baptism and the laying on of hands was a key element in the ritual of call and vocation. Those who participated understood that they were a part of a greater narrative and that their work was to go and do as Jesus had gone and done.

The sending and going of the first apostles is highlighted in the scripture by the story in Acts 8. The disciples in Jerusalem heard about other communities and baptisms taking place and they went to be with those people to pray for them and lay hands on them (Acts 8:14–17). We know there were people going out from Antioch who were prophets and teachers of Jesus's way (Acts 14:1). The community of shalom was not interested in power and authority. In fact, the apostles rejected this outright. Perhaps keeping in mind Jesus's words that they were not to be slaves to one another but friends, they did things differently (John 15:15). For instance, when it came time for the twelve to renew their number, they did not want any one person to be an overseer of another (Acts 1:21). There is some sense that the original twelve was an important group for discernment and they kept this number intact. Being connected to that group of friends centered in Jerusalem was important for Paul, and after his conversion he went to them about his mission and vocation (Acts 9:20). So while there was no formal structure to this growing community, and there are many communities, there was some sense that the original twelve are a crucial part of each community's work of discernment (Acts 2:41). The result of their work is the many Christian communities spread across the Mediterranean Basin by the early second century. These communities were neither linked nor unified. In other words, there was a universal or catholic mission, but there was no universal or catholic Church in terms of a shared structure.

The book of Acts documents very little formal instruction being handed down from the core leaders of the early Church in Jerusalem. The New Testament had not yet been written. There was no teacher/student pedagogy, or a formation-based model of instruction. Literacy was a privilege in the first century so few had access to the Old Testament. Most everyone depended upon others to either know the stories or be able to read the stories for them. We do know that some communities kept non-standardized caches of letters and Jesus sayings that would eventually form the nexus of the New Testament. This was predominately a movement of untrained uninformed people sharing their understanding of God's vision of a peaceful community in this world and the next. They took their place in the narrative and went where they were invited to create communities of peace. While Christians in Jerusalem were rehearsing the things they remembered about their time with Jesus, what about the communities further afield? Perhaps they too cherished and recited sayings and stories people picked up about Jesus and his way. Based upon what we have said already, it is clear these teachings urged the churches to continue the work of making peaceful communities,[9] and this work was the paradigm for the heavenly inheritance of the Resurrection. They believed the shalom formed here would last into the end times.

One of the single most important teachings was the death of Christ and his Resurrection, by which Christians would receive resurrection and could experience the freedom from sin portended by the resurrection in their communities of peace now. While other religious people of the time had many forms of spirituality and ideas about heaven, it appears as if, in these informal sharing moments of teaching across the universal experience of the early Christian movement, there was a great commitment to the good news that God had died and was resurrected. There was very little wavering on this at all.[10] In fact, we are told that when the people heard of the freedom obtained by Jesus's victimhood and God's mighty act of death's own death resulting in resurrection, they were added daily to the movement of peace (Acts 2:41).

The other part of the early Church's gathering was a meal. We liturgically oriented people are very quick to say, "Look! See, there is the Eucharist," but that is reading back into history the expectation that what we do in all our various forms across the Church today is what Jesus did at the Last Supper, and what the variety of early Christians did in response to Jesus's command to remember these things. Unfortunately, it is not that simple. It is widely accepted that early Christians cherished certain key traditions; for instance, the story of the Last Supper itself was familiar and was used liturgically during mealtimes at regular gatherings of the faithful. We see these formulas and traditions echoed in both the Gospels and in the letters of the New Testament.[11] However, the kind of liturgical standardization that happened in the third century was still a ways off. Christians did not celebrate just one single kind of shared meal, and the words of institution from the Last Supper were not universally employed at meals shared among the early churches.[12] What is clear is that those who went on God's behalf, accepting God's mission of making communities of peace, did not simply rehearse the ministry of Jesus, but they also shared food with others. The common meal was an essential characteristic of the community shared among the people Jesus first called and sent. The early writings of the Church made clear that such a common meal was clearly essential in Jesus's own ministry.

The earliest followers of Jesus did what he taught them to do: they gathered, gave thanks, broke the bread and gave to each other, and then did the same with the wine—more often they shared regular meals. The theological gloss that the shared meal is a remembrance of Christ's sacrifice for atonement was not established until the third century. In the book of Acts we see the disciples living out their remembrance of what Jesus did. I draw here on scholarship around the repetitive action of the *chabûrah*, or the feast of friends. It is very popular to combine the ancient "giving thanks" we find in Acts with the Seder meal, connecting both to the Passover. This connection is not quite accurate. Jesus's custom was to eat with all kinds of people—the righteous and the unrighteous alike. His custom was to celebrate the feast of friends. Such transgressive meals most likely hastened his death. Jesus's breaking of bread also broke open social, religious, and political customs. Dom Gregory Dix points out that the *chabûrah* is what teachers and disciples ate together. The Eucharist originated with this feast of friends, rather than with the Passover Seder! It was not until the time of ninth century that Alcuin introduces the Passover elements into the Eucharistic feast.[13]

It is important to note that neither the Passover symbolism, nor the connection of baptism to the Eucharist originated with the earliest Church. Both of these "givens" of Eucharistic practice were not part of Jesus's nor the early church's traditions. They arrive into our customary later, in the midst of a drastic change in the role of the clergy. This change eroded Jesus's tradition of gathering people together for a feast of friends that bound one another into the community of shalom. Before the feast of friends became the Mass, a diverse community of peace gathered at table, just as Jesus had, and gave thanks for what they had been given and what they were yet to receive. They remembered that the meal was provided by God and for the journey, and they shared it with others. The community of peace, as we said in the last chapter, was a community that fed people. Luke writes, "Day by day, as they spent much time together in the temple, they broke bread at home and ate their food with glad and generous hearts" (Acts 2:46).

The last quality of the apostolic shalom community worthy of note is their practice of sharing what they had. They shared the good news of Jesus's resurrection and of the community and reign of peace. They shared the Holy Spirit (Acts 8:14). They did mighty works to be sure (Acts 3:1–7). All of this required no repayment. It was free to anyone who desired to be a member of the peace community and rejected the dominion of violence and a world where fees were charged for service. There was no enrichment to be had in this endeavor of mission. We do know that this mixed community of the poor and the wealthy came together to share what they had so that all might have what they needed to live. Those who lived together in community (which may have been the twelve and their families) shared things in common (Acts 2:42). Everyone in the community sold their possessions and placed their funds in a common purse for the good of all (Acts 4:34–35). This was a key ingredient to belonging to the community in Jerusalem, so much so that they confronted those who did not trust the community or God fully and did not give over all that they had (Acts 5:1–11). This is important because the community in Jerusalem, as a paradigm, understood that everything had to be pooled together and used for the good of the whole. It had to be redistributed. In still other parts of the movement, different ways were used to take in money and redistribute it for the good of all. In the case of Lydia, or the centurion in Acts, no requirement was made that they sell everything. At the core was an understanding that it was good to give and share what one had (Hebrews 13:15–16).

Those who followed God in the community of shalom rejected the norms of consumption, wealth, and the oppression of the poor. They rejected the economic system of the day in favor of a community of peace where there was no hunger. The care of the needy among the Church was so important that the first "ministers" called into the fledgling community were tasked with caring for those who could not take care of themselves: the widows and orphans who were being neglected in the distribution of food (Acts 6:1–6). The early Church's rule of life was a direct indictment of the practice of the religious authorities. And the early Church wasted no time telling the authorities that they should feed these people. They simply fed the people. When the community of peace shares what they have with those who are going without, they undermine the powers and authorities that prey upon the weak, needy, and vulnerable and hold them up as scapegoats for society's problems.

The story of the conversion of Saul, who became Paul, displays the adaptable custom of this new community. Paul's experience echoes Jesus's story of the Good Samaritan (Luke 10:25–37) and shows that the early church was struggling to stretch its boundaries and adapt for the sake of its mission. Paul is mentioned early on in Acts during the martyrdom of Stephen. He held the cloaks of those who killed Stephen (Acts 7:54–60; Acts 22:20). He participated in the punishment of those in the new movement that had organized around Jesus. Paul persecuted members of the shalom community (1 Cor. 15:8–10). He ravaged the gatherings of Christians and dragged people off to prison (Acts 8:3). He used violence to bring about conformity within his religious tradition (Acts 9:1). He saw the new movement of peace that lived on in the name of Jesus as a threat to the established powers of the day, and he used violence to try and crush the movement. Paul was no friend of the Church, and he did all he could to keep the movement from taking root.

En route to Damascus on a mission to capture followers of Jesus, Paul had a conversion experience.[14] The living Word invited Paul to set aside his violence. He was struck blind and made very weak. While the man on the road to Jericho in Jesus's parable is a victim of violence, Paul was a victimizer of others. Before the throne of God and with the consequences of his violent actions revealed, Paul fell to the ground.[15] The men by his side did nothing.[16] There was a community member nearby named Ananias. His allegiance to Jesus made him a religious outsider like the good Samaritan.[17] Ananias was called by God to heal Paul and bring him into the community of peace. Ananias did not think Paul had a place in the community of peace because of the evil he had done to the Church. God reminded Ananias that the community was not responsible for the call; God was, and God had called this murderous, violent man into service.[18] Moreover, God intended to use Paul to carry God's mission to the ends of the earth and far beyond the boundaries of his comfort.[19] Like the Samaritan in Jesus's parable, Ananias crossed the boundary of infamy that surrounded Paul and created a new community of peace between the two of them. He took pity on Paul and set aside his reservations about Paul's worth and character.[20] He healed Paul of his blindness.[21] Ananias did what the followers of the way do. He restored Paul's health by laying hands upon him. He baptized Paul. Ananias entered Paul's suffering and befriended him, knowing that his reputation among the wider Church would suffer. The Samaritan gave up comfort, spent money, and enabled the healing of the man he found in the ditch. He entered the ditch and joined the man in his suffering. Through his compassion, the Samaritan became the neighbor of the man.[22] Like the Samaritan, Ananias and his community paid extravagantly to bring Paul into their community. They shared a common cup and broke bread. Paul regained his strength and learned the rhythms of the community of peace.[23]

As we know, Paul's mission was profoundly shaped by the way God called him and invited him to reject his life of violence to take on the yoke of peace. Paul became the voice of God to the Gentiles and all those in the wider community who had no place in the inheritance of Israel. Paul began to proclaim that God's narrative of grace, begun with Abraham and Sarah, was meant for all people.[24]

Paul's conversion was actually the reconversion of the community of shalom. The community was reminded to be different from other religious communities, and different from the powers and authorities of the world. The community did not repay violence with violence, but practiced peace instead. Theologian Ivan Illich sees in the story of the Samaritan what we see in the story of Ananias: "A faith in the incarnate word sacrificed on the cross [that] is not a religion and cannot be analyzed with the concepts of religious science." Ananias rejected the commonly held value of vengeance in order to embrace Paul.[25] Ananias took a "step fearlessly outside what his culture [had] sanctified in order to create a new relationship and, potentially, a new community. He [did] not seek God within a sacred circle but [found] him lying by the road in a ditch."[26]

Ananias's story reveals that the gospel of peace did not take root as a new written code about baptism, laying on of hands, teaching, Eucharist, or sharing goods in a new economy. Instead, Ananias's actions demonstrated that the community of peace was a new life with God as a part of an ancient, overarching narrative of forgiveness. His actions echo Paul's second letter to the Corinthians, "You yourselves are our letter, written on our hearts, to be known and read by all; and you show that you are a letter of Christ, prepared by us, written not with ink but with the Spirit of the living God, not on tablets of stone but on tablets of human hearts" (2 Cor. 3:2–3). Ananias and Paul were both invited to become a new community that rejected the necessity of violence against one another. We are invited by God into a new life—not a new code. The Christian movement undoes religion itself.

The first apostles ventured out declaring that God had undone the religion of vengeance, just as God did between Ananias and Paul. They went from Jerusalem and Galilee to Samaria, Caesarea, Antioch, Laodicea Cyprus, Perga, Pisidian Antioch, Asia Minor, and Greece. High points included Jerusalem, Tiberias, Caesarea Philippi, Damascus, Antioch, Tarsus, Pisidian Antioch, Troas, Philippi, Thessolonica, Beroea, Piraes, Athens, Corinth, Ephesus, Miletus, Cnidus, and Rodhos. They went to Crete and Sicily and to Rome. In each of these places we see footprints of the movement of peace and the creation of multiple types of Christian communities. Scripture and early writings reveal that the early movement of peace sprouted in the towns of Galilee and in Nazareth.[27] Many of these groups were ejected from the synagogues, but the culture of the synagogue remained important to this particular kind of Christian community. Unused or abandoned synagogues were often reinhabited by Christians. Some of the church buildings began their lives as synagogues, some of which we have learned about from Paul's letters and from archeological digs are Duro Europos, Stobi, and Delos.[28]

People also met in homes, which is clear from the letters of Paul to the different communities. He connected and networked a variety of house churches overseen by women and men. These house churches made up the urban side of the early Christian experience, and they were often connected to other associations and societies. There were clusters of communities that gathered together throughout a whole association, popularized through particular associations of artisans, for example. New Testament scholar Wayne Meeks argues that such associations broke open family clusters and disrupted systems of belonging. Schools were another kind of Christian community. Similar to philosophical schools of the day, followers of Jesus gathered around a particular teacher or noted leader. The disciples met together, learned together, and debated one another. These learning groups included professionals and students. Discourse and guidance given to the disciples were part of the unique nature of these groups. They grew, and some of these schools became distinct church communities.[29]

While the cities swelled with a variety of Christian communities, rural churches also thrived. After Jesus's resurrection, communities of cave-dwelling desert fathers were established, along with small groups of praying women and communes filled with people who believed in separating themselves from society to prepare for Jesus's return. The latter foreshadowed monastic orders. I have outlined some of the diverse forms of early church communities we know about, but there were unquestionably more. Multiple communities lived and died in this very formative fifty- to one-hundred-year period of the early Church.[30]

The first people of this community of shalom were not passive bystanders to the vocation of their community. They were not making personal pietistic commitments to do good things. They were active participants in the story of Israel's being raised out of bondage and Jesus's rising from the dead. They did not meet in conclaves to raise a fist against "the man" and the powers that be. Their prophetic judgment was making a community of shalom. The very existence of their communities judged the world of human violence without raised voices or finger-wagging activism.[31] There was no private faith offered as a choice among many communities. Their collaborative mission resisted the impulse to distill the church into a boundaried set of relationships based upon forms of natural law or holiness codes.[32]

The Christian Church often looks back on itself from outside of the story of Israel. When it does, it misses that the first Christians were not about a "new" thing, but a very ancient thing. God calls people into community to be as God is—a holy community. Christians become like Christ by participating in an overarching narrative from the past. There is no second option here. We must risk our boundaries, eat with sinners, and love them as our own siblings, regardless of what the religious or political powers tell us. Christ's death makes us members and citizens of the reign of peace. Baptism reminds us publicly that we are recipients of God's grace. Israel's narrative has been written and our names a part of it. The laying on of hands calls us into this ancient mission. We take on new lives, new clothes, as adaptations of Christ himself. We have the community of apostles to guide us and Christ as our foundation. Whatever we do, we are sign and symbol of life lived in Christ Jesus. The world is in "fundamental rebellion," using systems of power, authority, and violence to maintain its fallen-ness.[33] The community of shalom reveals this truth by its communal foundation in the life and narrative of Israel and Christ.

The community of peace is a body of people equal in mission and ministry, and one part of the long arc of God's salvation narrative. Our story is embedded in this ancient story. The early Church understood that they were perpetuating the kingdom of shalom. All too soon, these basic elements of God's shalom community would be bent to the powers and authorities of the world. The habits of the communities of peace in the first years following the Resurrection faded as the apostles succumbed to power, and became subject to the age-old sibling rivalry that fuels institutions and perpetuates cycles of violence.

CHAPTER FIVE

Detour toward Principality

Emergence Christians are allergic to real estate because, they will say, "The minute you own a piece of real estate, then you have to have somebody to clean it, then you have to have somebody to be sure that it gets clean, then you have to get somebody to be sure that it's insured, and the next thing you know, you've got a bishop."

—Phyllis Tickle[1]

The primitive community of peace was a movement of God's people. In the beginning it traveled light and depended upon the hospitality of a diverse group of friends; it did not depend upon institutional structures. Its diversity and lack of structure made it adaptive. It had no overhead and existed by the kindness of benefactors—the wealthy, and those who opened their homes and shared a scrap of bread. Jesus easily fits into modern categories of a refugee (Matt. 2:13–23), a homeless person (Luke 9:3), and an itinerant beggar (Mark 6:10). The earliest movement of what would be called Christianity mimicked Christ in these ways. Their missionary community was free from the bondage of economies of state, religion, powers, and authorities. Over time many joined those first hundred men and women that Jesus sent out (Luke 10). There was a wide diversity of communities and community leaders.

Raymond Brown indicates that there was a great sense of unity in the apostolic Church. There were theological differences between the different communities, but they were unified around the importance of their wider mission and the story of God's call and invitation.[2] As the movement grew, so did the need to deal with differences, authority, and tradition. The Church became a principality.

Part of our work is to sort out the changes and understand how we arrived at today's Church. We look back hoping to spur reform. Yet, from a faithful perspective, we must also accept that we have made it thus far because of the institutional structures we have innovated. A fellow bishop is fond of saying, "Every movement gets organized or it dies." Today we are writing the next chapter of the story. Our churches have withstood the test of time through structure and organization. Many good things have come to us because of the Church's work as the vessel and first fruits of the reign of peace. We have created ways of forming both the baptized and leaders so that the Church might call and invite ever new generations into the work of shalom.

In the first century after Christ's resurrection, there was a formalization of community life. Informal communal connections and relationships generated new norms and practices. We have surveyed the diverse, living, growing, thriving life of these early communities. It was the risen Lord, their relationships with each other, and their commitment to bring about the kingdom of shalom that united them. Archeological evidence reveals that commonplace objects, common places, and common people were the primary locus of the relational act of gathering. There were few assigned roles, if any. These gatherings and associations were an ad hoc enterprise. All members of the community shared in the communal life and were free to speak and teach, prophesy and serve.[3]

Undermining the prevailing economies of power and wealth was essential to the success of the new communities of peace. They shared what they had freely and served others. The church in Jerusalem had a radical form of communal organization that emphasized the sharing of gifts and the pooling of money. This was not characteristic of all early Christian communities. Nevertheless, there was a universal concern for the poor. Paul's letters reveal that it was routine to take up collections for the poor and to share resources among and between the churches. Acts details the sharing of money to care for widows and orphans. In his letter to the Galatians, Paul writes that it is the main mission of the church to provide for those in need and those outside their community (Gal. 2:10). The Christian community that lifted up the letter of James understood that the primary focus of Jesus's ministry and the primary recipients of the gospel were the poor (James 2:5). Early Christians were widely known to serve the poor. The early Church believed that tending the poor, housing the oppressed, and feeding the hungry were the work of the gospel.

Conflict often arose in these early communities, and the apostles intervened to give advice. Paul's letters are filled with such counsel. But their words were never intended to set universal norms. These letters do not provide a complete and total picture of the apostolic Church. Given the informal nature of the network of Christian house churches, there was a lot of diverse practice between communities. Furthermore, the New Testament does not record any formal training being required of those who led the small and growing Christian communities. There was no vocational discernment. Everyone shared in the work of the whole body. Information was passed on in an organic, informal way. Wisdom was shared through stories, prayers, and hymns and all of the faithful were encouraged in the work of going to others on God's behalf. They were invited to take up the cross and walk in the way of peace and humility. The first-century hymn preserved in Paul's letter to the Philippians gives us a taste of this:

> Let the same mind be in you which is in Christ Jesus,
> who, though he was in the form of God,
> did not regard equality with God
> as something to be exploited,
> but emptied himself,
> taking the form of a slave,
> being born in human likeness.
> And being found in human form,
> he humbled himself

and became obedient to the point of death—
even death on a cross.
Therefore God also highly exalted him
and gave him the name
that is above every name,
so that at the name of Jesus
every knee should bend,
in heaven and on earth and under the earth,
and every tongue should confess
that Jesus Christ is Lord,
to the glory of God the Father. (Phil. 2:5–11)[4]

Leaders were chosen through prayer and discernment. The remaining disciples cast lots to choose who would replace Judas in Jerusalem (Acts 1:26). Many Church historians surmise that there was a focus on the gifts and fruits of the Spirit, which is evident in the writings of Paul where he bears witness to the leadership qualities necessary for community.[5] But even these gifts were quite a fluid basis for recognizing authority. The New Testament offers no instruction on how to know the fruits of the Spirit or how to discern them. There is also no instruction on how to use them for specific tasks. It is difficult to see such a description of gifts as a prescription for organizing community. In fact, there is no real instruction in the scripture about how to do so. The scriptures focus on the call and invitation, the going and what one might do, and the invitation to make community and be a blessing of peace to the world. While we are in the habit of expounding on the leadership qualities of Jesus or the disciples, such modern understandings of individual leadership were simply not part of how the New Testament authors understood the Church.

These early communities of peace had become primarily an urban movement by the beginning of the second century. Whatever momentum had been gained in Nazareth and Galilee seems to have dissipated during this period. Perhaps the central focus on urban mission, the fact that more people lived closely together in cities, and the realities of subsistence living in rural areas contributed to the early Church's urban orientation.[6] This period occasioned a seismic shift in tradition. Communities stopped remembering the Last Supper in the midst of the *chabûrah*, the feast of friends. The service of thanksgiving took on a life of its own as the Eucharist. The Church was transformed by new contexts. The limitless boundaries of Jesus, who would eat with anybody, were slowly lost in practice, perhaps out of fear of discovery during persecution, perhaps out of a desire for theological orthodoxy, or perhaps out of a desire for keeping the community small. The nature of the feast changed from a gathering of the friends and acquaintances of Jesus to a service for the select few. The celebration of the Eucharist remained in house church settings for the most part, though communities also met in cemeteries, prisons, and tombs of the martyrs. Fasting, prayer, and prophecy were part of the life of the Christian in this period.[7] There was a rise in infant baptism because most Christians were now being born into the community.[8] Despite low literacy rates and the predominately flat nature of the community, the movement accumulated stores of letters, narratives, and documents. The majority of this quickly growing body of Christian literature was not authored by clergy or trained philosophers.[9]

The Christian communities continued to undermine economies of violence by caring for the elderly, widows, orphans, prisoners, and the shipwrecked.[10] They also supported families who had lost loved ones because of their faith during the persecutions. The early Church maintained a reputation for caring for people who were not part of the community. Pagan emperor Julian confessed, "The godless Galileans feed not only their poor but ours as well." The early Church leader Tertullian (CE 155–220) wrote:

> Each of us puts in a trifle on the monthly day, or when he pleases; but only if he pleases, and only if he is able, for no man is obliged, but contributes of his own free will. These are, as it were, deposits of piety; for it is not paid out thence for feasts and drinking and thankless eating houses, but for feeding and burying the needy, for boys and girls deprived of means and parents, for old folk now confined to the house: also for them that are shipwrecked, for any who are in the mines, and for any who, in the islands, or in the prisons, if only it be for the cause of God's people.[11]

The community members shared what they had. Because they gathered in homes and public spaces, there was little overhead for the mission. There were few employed leaders, so the economic cost of the work was relatively low.[12] Almsgiving was the keystone of Christian discipleship. People supported the common purse of the community and the poor. In a letter from the second century, Clement wrote, "Almsgiving is good even as penitence for sin: fasting is better than prayer, but the giving of alms is better than both."[13]

His letter indicates a first step in theologizing the work of the gospel. Giving alms had become a means for forgiveness. The Church inaugurated an economy where certain actions (fasting, prayer, or almsgiving) were a means of receiving forgiveness of sin. Such transactions of faith undermined the nature of earlier shalom communities where all were welcome and invited to share what they had in a remaking of creation. As the Church began to view fasting, prayer, and almsgiving as income that earned forgiveness, it organized an internal economy focused on the salvation of souls. Such an economy was foreign to the tradition of Sinai and the vision of Jesus. In fact, Jesus forgave, healed, and fed without the primacy of an offering. This step into the economy of salvation moved the Church on to the slippery slope of principality making.

As the system of Church began to form, it became necessary to establish a process of formation. The Church became focused on preparing the baptized for the vocation of the ministry. Christian philosophical schools emerged around people like Justin Martyr, one of the first Christian apologists, who was gifted in the theology of the Word. These philosophical schools remained few in number and did not provide regular training for ministers. They were ad hoc groups of people gathered around a teacher.

There were also early catechetical schools,[14] which were historically significant, though short lived in the scope of church history. The first Christians were predominately Jews or "God fearers"—Gentiles—who knew the faith of Israel already and believed in one God. Because these early converts were already familiar with Jewish tradition, people could be brought into the community through baptism and empowered by the laying on of hands rather quickly. However, as the Church diversified further, it became necessary to teach the basics of the faith. Scholars believe that the first catechumenate ministries emerged in the middle of the second century. Justin makes mention of the movement in one of his first letters.[15] The catechumenate could last up to two years. It preceded baptism and the laying on of hands. In some cases, there may also have been a verbal and public set of questions asked prior to baptism.[16] When I graduated from seminary in the 1990s, these catechetical schools were viewed as the normative way for entering early Christian community. That is not true. There were many kinds of baptismal preparations during the period in question; the catechumenate simply had the benefit of being mentioned in the few letters that remain from the second century.

Another form of early Christian formation is captured in texts like *The Didache*, a second-century tool for instruction after baptism. It was a scroll kept in the community meeting house, just as the Torah scrolls were kept in the synagogue. The leaders of the community might read from it from time to time, perhaps in the liturgy of the community. It is unlikely that every Christian house church or synagogue church even had a copy of *The Didache* or something like it, though scholars believe it was widely circulated. We have examples of *The Didache* in Greek, Syriac, Latin, Coptic, and Arabic.[17] Despite questions about its ubiquity, *The Didache* is important for understanding the formation of Christians in the second century and beyond. About a third of the text serves as a primer for baptism. The other two-thirds are devoted to instruction for church leaders and those who are new and already baptized. "Athanasius describes it as 'appointed by the Fathers to be read by those who newly join us.'"[18] It includes teachings on how to fast and pray. It has lessons on baptism and the Lord's Supper. It also talks about leadership, church officers, and who is to be trusted. It has some discussion of the life of the community. Crucially, during this phase of Christian community, most Christian formation happened *after* baptism.

The Didache does proscribe some basic instruction prior to baptism:

> This is how to baptize. Give public instruction on all these points, and then "baptize" in running water, "in the name of the Father and of the

Son and of the Holy Spirit." . . . If you do not have running water, baptize in some other. If you cannot in cold, then in warm. If you have neither, then pour water on the head three times "in the name of the Father, Son, and Holy Spirit." Before the baptism, moreover, the one who baptizes and the one being baptized must fast, and any others who can. And you must tell the one being baptized to fast for one or two days beforehand.[19]

Before baptism a neophyte learned to share what they have with others. The person was to be guileless, humble, and good. They were to refrain from adultery, lying, theft, blasphemies, idolatry, lust, pedophilia, sex, and evil deeds—a kind of basic set of commandments. The individual was also to be a servant to all and obedient to authority.[20]

Like Clement's formulary for almsgiving and fasting, *The Didache* was a point along the line of the Church's development into a formalized and organized community. With increasing conflict between various Christian communities, a catechetical document had become necessary. Despite Jesus's prayer that we all might be one, and his willingness to speak in parables instead of doctrine, the Church was drawn into theological sibling rivalry. During this period, the orders of ministry began to coalesce and their distinctiveness was more visible. We have the seeds of hierarchy. People were invited to serve as president at the Eucharist and administer the ministry.[21] The letters of Ignatius indicate that duties were parsed out. *The Didache* suggests that those who do the work of apostleship, prophecy, and teaching be selected based upon the gifts given by the Spirit.[22] Ignatius and his fellow bishops were what we think of as "cardinal rectors" today. They oversaw the growing urban communities and dealt with discipline, money, and the laying on of hands.[23] They received no special training for this work. They were simply individuals who appeared gifted for the work and were raised up. Liturgically bishops were the ordinary ministers of the Eucharist assisted by presbyters. Over time the celebration of the Eucharist got refocused on the priesthood, thus associating the Eucharist with priesthood rather than with the episcopate, and thus leading to the bishop as priest with specialized non-Eucharistic functions.[24]

Alistair Stewart argues that the role of bishop was focused on the worldly and economic affairs of the growing Christian movement. Essentially, the bishop was the priest who took care of the business. The mono-episcopacy grew out of federations of churches specifically in Rome. Its emergence in Rome and Asia (it seems *not* to emerge in Jerusalem) brought about the three-fold order with an emphasis on the episcopal see as the central hub of organization.[25] Their work was the same as their counterparts in Roman society. The early Christian writers described the bishop's ministry as the collection and distribution of common funds. Bishops provided money for ministry. They also oversaw marriages, grappled with heresy, saw that slaves did not spend church money incorrectly, and ensured that the poor got relief.[26] The word used to describe the office of bishop was interchangeable with the word used for "presbyter." In the earliest period of the three orders of ministry, the labels were job titles more than separate ordained offices.

This time period provides the earliest examples of ordination in ancient texts. What is clear, without exception, is that people were ordained by prayer. The ritual sign of that prayer was the laying on of hands. After the prayer and the laying on of hands, they were given the particular work of celebrating or administering.[27] Despite the emergence of these defined roles in the life of the Church, at the end the second century the Church still had a very flat, ad hoc approach to leadership and organization.

In the third century, the shape of the Church became more recognizable. Christianity came out into public space, and, though persecutions continued, the number of communities could no longer be hidden. They grew larger and larger. The homes of the wealthy were used for Eucharist and the vessels were beautiful. The ordinary vessels for bread and wine reminiscent of the feast of friends were discarded in favor of more ornate items. By the end of the third century, buildings were built to house Christian celebrations. These spaces were increasingly organized around an altar.[28] Music and scripture readings became normative. Not everyone agreed on what should be read, so the third century was a period of great debate over what books should be in the Bible, and over sticky theological questions like the nature of Jesus. A debate raged over the Triune God, and the budding church needed a means of exerting control.[29]

Christians were out in the open. There were Christian senators and the Church was represented in the higher social classes. Very few slaves still belonged to the movement. Many of the Christians were part of the "free classes." They were citizens. Women, especially women of high status, were key to the Church's life and ministry. In the past, Christians had not participated in public life for fear of idolatry. Christians now began to enter into these festivals.[30] By the end of the third century, the Christian movement was moving into the role of one principality among others.

Gregory the Illuminator (257–331) tells us that clergy in rural communities were fed, as the Levitical priests had been, from the abundance of sacrifice. In Carthage, bishops controlled the common purse and made distributions to clergy and for their own expenses. Historian Henry Chadwick says that by 251, the common purse in Rome was supporting the bishop, forty-six presbyters, seven deacons, seven subdeacons, forty-two acolytes, and fifty-two exorcists, readers, and doorkeepers, along with more than fifteen hundred widows and needy persons. The Roman Church was generous and shared with poorer regions. They supported other bishops in foreign lands and safeguarded refugee bishops. This kind of generosity was unknown in the world at this time.[31] Such growth in centralized collection, the support of the clergy, and the formalization of systems of hospitality and care for the poor were a huge step in the Church's transition into a principality. No longer was hospitality to the stranger or almsgiving for the poor a matter of economic confrontation with the powers that be; a whole theological and economic system was operational.

The Didache continued as a standard form of instruction through this period and for several hundred more years. The basics of the faith from the second period of postapostolic formation were affirmed in a later document called *The Apostolic Constitutions*, which dates from the middle of the fourth century—perhaps 325.[32] It added a few more essential theological formularies. The catechumens were taught about God as Trinity. The new converts learned about creation and then about the prophets of the Old Testament. They were to live piously, as *The Didache* recommended.[33] The catechumenate continued to expand in duration as well. Hippolytus advised an instruction period of three years for the newly baptized.[34] Over three hundred years, Christian formation had developed into a three-year time of strict preparation, instruction, fasting, exorcism, and prayer. This development paralleled the movement of Christianity from a self-organizing movement to an established institution, and the movement from a time of disbursed communities and a diversity of teachings, through a time of persecution and the great internal quarrels over heresies, to a time of centralized doctrinal control. The more Christianity became established, the more control became necessary.

By the middle of the third century, each Christian community of any means had a bishop at its center. At least in the East, these places with bishops in residence were called a *diocese*. In Egypt alone, there were over one hundred bishops and jurisdictions by the fourth century. The western and northern edges of the Church had fewer bishops, and were more spread out with wider dioceses to oversee.[35] The fourth-century diocese closely resembled the Roman government structure. The church modeled its organization after the Roman imperial cult. The term *Pontifex maximus* was used in reference to the bishop of Rome.

After settling into the habit of mimicking state geography and organization, dioceses remained largely unchanged. Bishops were supported by a host of presbyters, priests, and deacons. New churches were founded and bishops were put in place to oversee their growth and ministry. The evolution moved from every church having a bishop to the bishop having oversight of priests and deacons who oversaw the local work at the church when the bishop was not present. The role of the bishop shifted from being a leader of a single church to being a geographic apostolic representative.

Suffice it to say, the *ecclesia*, the community of peace, imagined on the Galilean seashore had changed. Like a pebble tossed in a pond with ever expanding ripples, the emergence of Christianity in the urban centers of the Roman Empire forced the Church to adopt new forms and structures for mission and ministry. Jesus's movement became a thriving principality. At the close of the third century, an organized Church had replaced a disorganized but single-minded community on a mission of peace. The Church was experiencing exponential growth. There was a wide variety of church work, but most of it was still done by the baptized and not the clergy. Lay preachers, teachers, apologists, community leaders, and all manner of other ministries streamed forth from the Christian community into the wider, still mostly nonbelieving, society. Formation was incredibly varied. There were philosophical schools, monks, catechetical ministries, and a growing library of resources. Creeds were created and a Bible was canonized. The wider culture began to accept Christians as leaders. The Church was known for its service and its care for the poor. There were many types of communities. The third century was an important era because the Church of that time maintained both the formal and informal tools of mission. We have much to learn from the third-century Church about how to form vocations around mission, how to hold our structures lightly, and how to embrace a diverse set of communities.

CHAPTER SIX

The Church Principality

Life is an unfoldment, and the further we travel the more truth we can comprehend. To understand the things that are at our door is the best preparation for understanding those that lie beyond.

—Hypatia of Alexandria[1]

Hypatia was a woman, a pagan, and a philosopher (c. 370–415). She was killed by a Christian mob known as the Parabalani. She had been drawn into a conflict between Orestes, the prefect of Alexandria, and Cyril, the bishop of Alexandria. It was a fight over faith, power, and the best way to govern. Orestes made a report following her death and resigned. Cyril spread the rumor that she had moved to Athens and there had been no mob and no tragedy.[2]

Hypatia died because sibling rivalry, that willingness to kill because of difference, had infected the Christian movement. With the exception of Judas's betrayal,[3] the movement had been rather peaceful, maintaining a substantial countercultural momentum through the third century. But as the movement institutionalized, the Church began to jockey for power. The fourth century was a time of momentous change in the Church: the inauguration of a thousand years of institutional power and strength. The Church became a premiere principality and authority and began to employ violence strategically. Almost overnight, the Roman Empire became nominally Christian under Constantine, largely due to his mother, Helena.

Church and state begin a long and tangled love affair. By the end of the
fourth century, the Roman Empire had adopted Christianity as its official
religion. Theological sibling rivalry fueled a long history of the Church
persecuting various kinds of dissenters as heretics.

The Church expanded in every way imaginable. Many churches were
built as the institution was allowed to own property. Christians also took
over pagan temples. The faith spread through missionary outreach to the
Germanic peoples and the migrant tribes of Northern Europe. These people were nothing like the Roman citizens who were schooled in Greek
philosophy, and missionaries were forced to adopt new methods to encour-
age conversion.[4]

The fourth century also marked the rise of monasticism. Monasteries
became an important incubator for theological education. Basil of Caesarea
and the Cappadocian Fathers innovated a scholastic approach to theology. The monastics also fostered a new missionary zeal. Irish monks and
scholars prepared a new generation of missionaries that travelled all over
Western Europe and the British Isles. They formed new monasteries and
sent out more missionaries. The Commune of Vaison (529) instructed
"every monastic priest to take a child under his care, teach him the Psalter,
liturgical rites and Christian morals 'to put [the child] in the way to succeed him.'"[5]

By the fifth century, the Church was rethinking its posture toward the
poor and marginalized. The rise of monasticism meant that the Church
had become the state's means of caring for the poor. The well-being of the
indigent population depended upon the diligence of the monks, priests,
and bishops. They carried out their acts of charity on behalf of the whole
society. Fifth-century churches included a diaconal area where deacons
collected and distributed alms and food for the poor. Deacons had a great
deal of power within the Church, but they were no longer the missionary
face of the Christian community in the world. They had become a fixture
within the Church hierarchy.

For laypeople, giving became a means of gaining distinction and earn-
ing virtue from the saints and God. People used their charitable gifts as a
justification for distancing themselves from the actual suffering of the poor.

Christian society began to differentiate on the basis of class. Almsgiving absolved the wealthy from the sin of owning private property.[6] The Church became the middleman between rich and poor. In Rome, a quarter of all church revenue went to the bishop. The remaining sum was divided among dependent clergy and the sick.[7]

The Church became so synonymous with the structures of the Empire that the mission of Jesus was only intermittently recognizable. Augustine imagined a Church unseen as a theological construct because it was becoming difficult to discern the kingdom of peace within the churchly principality that had grown out of Jesus's ad hoc society of friends. As baptism and liturgical participation became the office of every imperial citizen, even the emphasis on invitation and diversity was sidelined in favor of a forced uniformity that abandoned the table fellowship of the first apostles. As the "Christian" state oppressed others, raised armies, taxed, created laws, and accepted the trappings of power, Christians were confused about what the Church actually was in the world. The *Pax Christiana*, the peace of Christians, became identical to the *Pax Romana*: a peace won by the powerful with violence. This seems apparent to the theologians of the day.[8] In order to deal with the fallen nature of the Church, Augustine and others begin to ponder the idea of the invisible true Church. The world and Church were violent even though there were plenty of Christians. Before Constantine and the Church of the Empire, Christians had had to deal with the reality that the world of violence existed, and that God still ruled despite all evidence to the contrary. After *Pax Christiana*, Christians understood that Christ was ruler of all and Prince of Peace. At the same time, they had to deal with the reality of the Church's complicity in violence. Holding these two ideas in tension led to a notion that somewhere there was a church more connected to the shalom of Christ, a believing church—even if it was invisible. The Christian hope that God was bringing about peace and righteousness to transform the world was outranked by the preservation of power between church and state.[9]

When the Roman Empire fell to invading armies, society turned to the Church for support. Fifth-century bishops Leo I and Gregory I were statesmen and public administrators, raising armies, taxing, and overseeing the mission and teaching of the Church. After Rome was sacked, the Church was the state. In the eastern part of the Empire, where the civil order remained intact, bishops did not take on the same powers as in the West. But in the West, the mingling of episcopal and civic authority grew ever more profound. Bishops served as chancellors and heads of the court throughout the monarchies that grew up from the ruins of the Western Roman Empire.

Clergy in the fifth century were generally not well educated, despite their august positions. Only a select few gained an education and participated at the highest levels of governance. Many bishops were consecrated entirely because of their gifts in administration. Laypeople and local clergy learned about what was going on around them through letters or books.[10] The catechumenate receded from view, as did all the second-century emphasis on the formation of the baptized.

The sixth century was an age where people created idiosyncratic local cults devoted to various Christian martyrs and saints. Buildings accrued particular status, and people made pilgrimages to famous shrines and churches. Despite the institutionalization of the Church, there was a wide variation among Christian buildings and liturgies. People built basilicas that were large and public. Liturgies in these grandiose spaces were large public rituals. While these liturgies were intended to support the faith of believers, they were also meant for "inquirers, the curious, or even its critics."[11] Attendance at these services was obligatory, though that hardly meant that everyone went. Household Eucharistic celebrations and their common vessels became obsolete. Books and vessels and vestments became essential aspects of worship.[12] Hymnody grew, as did the spectacle of the divine service. Spoken and sung words were operatic experiences that were events in and of themselves, besides communicating Christian history and theology. These changes inaugurated a two-century trajectory that led to an ordinary and common form of the Mass. The divine service began to look like what we celebrate today.[13]

New theologies of liturgy also emerged. Theological concepts revolving around God's sacrifice, Jesus as the Lamb, and the Atonement were woven into the body of the Mass. Where the bread broken among diverse friends in a home spoke of Jesus's mission of shalom, the evolving liturgy conveyed the principality of the Church. The Mass declared the Church's authority and legitimated its monopoly on truth. The Church had become a different kind of community.

As the role of the Mass grew in Christian life, the training of clergy became a serious issue. In 675, bishops gathered at the Council of Toledo demanded that clergy whose knowledge was deficient seek remedy for their ignorance. That such a declaration was necessary reveals the surprising fact that theological education was not a prerequisite for ordination. Most clergy simply did not study. Educated priests tended to work as clerks or in the administration of church or the state.[14]

During this phase, a major shift also took place regarding the Church's ordered vocations. In the early centuries, the orders of deacons, priests, and bishops all existed, but the relationships between them varied widely from place to place and were not always viewed hierarchically. In the latter part of the first millennium, however, a ladder of ascendancy began to develop that required one to pass through sequential orders, a process that was firmly in place by the middle of the tenth century. A long process of formation that included ministries such as doorkeeper, reader, acolyte, and subdeacon (the highest of the unordained orders) culminated in ordination to the diaconate and the priesthood. The top of the ladder was the priesthood because of its association with the celebration of the eucharist.[15] The ladder stopped at the priesthood.

In the early centuries of the Church, there was not much demand for a hierarchy of ordained vocations. Neil Alexander tells a story about a bishop who asked the pope, "Holy Father, I need more priests to help and I haven't got any. How am I going to do this?" The pope wrote back and said, "What about your deacons?" The bishop replied, "No, the deacons are not going to give up their power to become priests." Deacons controlled the money, and had tremendous power as a result. The pope wrote back and said, "Well, in that case, just find yourself a good faithful acolyte and make him a priest." In this developing medieval theology of orders, the priesthood was central, not the episcopate.[16]

Medieval priests satisfied the contextual needs of local communities. As the Church grew, greater influence rested upon the one person in the community who could accomplish the one thing that the community had to have done: celebrating the Eucharist.[17] Clergy enjoyed ever increasing rights and privileges. The elevation of the Eucharist changed how the Church understood itself. By the High Middle Ages, the priesthood was one of the most powerful positions in most any local community. Priests confected the Eucharist and therefore constituted the Church. Everyone else, including other ordained people like deacons, did not have the capacity to do the only thing the Church urgently needed to have done.[18] This foregrounding of the priesthood reverberates even into our own millennium. We cannot understate the sweeping consequences of this change for the Church's vocation and formation. By the twentieth century, the Western Church had sidelined the baptized and neglected their formation almost completely.

In the eighth century, the Church underwent another economic shift. The tithe became a compulsory tax—a new invention for the Christian Church in the West. This tax was necessitated by the transfer of responsibility for the poor and indigent from the priest and bishop to the emerging institutions of hospitals and guilds.[19] Monasteries, however, retained their connection to the poor and indigent. By the end of this period, almost all the offerings went to support the institutional Church and very little of it benefited the poor, though sometimes in-gatherings on special days were used for relief. The increasing neglect of the poor indicated that both overhead and complexity were growing in the institutional Church. What began as a community of shalom that shared food, shelter, and money in order to reveal a reign of peace had become a massive institution determined to perpetuate itself.

A side effect of the growing "guild" of priests was a need for educational institutions. Local theological schools popped up across Europe, overseen by local bishops. They were sometimes called "bishop schools." By the Middle Ages, such schools flourished in Gaul, Canterbury, and York. They taught Greek, Latin, music, astronomy for the Church calendar, ecclesiastical law, and liturgy. By the ninth century, it was a requirement that every cathedral have a school.[20] These cathedral schools eventually overtook the monasteries in their educational importance for clergy, though the monasteries remained influential until the Reformation, especially in the rural areas. These new educational institutions were not interested in good pastoring, but in the study of truth. Their course of study was "philosophical" and "contemplative" in nature. The vast majority of baptized and rural clergy went untrained.[21]

In the twelfth century, a new technology was invented: contracts. They began as oaths taken between merchants and eventually became the basis for marriage. Correspondingly, infidelity became a crime. Ivan Illich writes, "The marriage oath legalizes love, and the sign becomes a juridical category. Christ came to free us from the law, but Christianity allowed the legal mentality to be brought into the very heart of love."[22] Church courts and secular courts were created and sin was criminalized based upon contractual principles. The conclusion of the Fourth Lateran Council of 1215 reads: "Every Christian, be they man or woman, will go once a year to their pastor and confess their sins or otherwise face the penalty of going to hell in a state of grievous sin."[23] Previously, confession had been a means of public expiation for notorious sins. Now the priest was a jurist with the power to forgive sin on a case-by-case basis. Local pastors became judge and jury for their community members. Laypeople were expected to present themselves to the Church court having examined their souls and actions. But individuals were also beginning to discover that they had an inner court, the *forum internum*, which was their conscience. New possibilities for self-determination and self-judgment planted the seeds of the Enlightenment.

The institutionalization of the Church and its legalization of moral offense opened the door to a society composed of individuals with a conscience. One's conscience became the record holder of all one's deeds, which was essential to the idea of keeping or breaking one's oath or violating a contract. Contractual living became the basis of the modern state and nation. Citizenship became a matter of conscience and choice. Citizens pledged themselves and their lives to their homeland.

A new kind of betrayal becomes possible, in the Incarnation of God in Christ Jesus the Christian is called to be faithful not to the gods, or

to the city's rules, but to a face, a person; and, consequently, the darkness he allows to enter him by breaking faith acquires a completely
new taste. This is the experience of sinfulness. It is an experience of
confusion in front of the infinitely good, but it always holds the possibility of sweet tears, which express sorrow and trust in forgiveness.
This dimension of very personal, very intimate failure is changed
through criminalization, and through the way in which forgiveness
becomes a matter of legal remission. Once the sinner is obligated
to seek legal remission of a crime, his sorrow and his hope in God's
mercy becomes a secondary issue. This legalization of love opens the
individual to new fears. . . . These fears are easily exploited.[24]

Paradoxically, the reformed churches embraced the criminalization of
sin and shifted toward individualism as a means of freeing people from
the onerous demands of the Church. The Church unwittingly propelled
Western society into secularism and inaugurated the immanent frame,
which remains our primary mindset in the West. Jesus endeavored to
free people from a centralized, hierarchical, religious system of laws that
benefited the few. As the Church became a principality, it created just
such a system.

CHAPTER SEVEN

A Modern Avocation

The Reformer is always right about what's wrong. However, he's often wrong about what is right.

—G. K. Chesterton[1]

As the Western world shifted into the modern age, the Church remained a great principality. It governed and managed significant resources. It was an economic force with the authority to tax, and clergy were subject to an independent judicial system. Bishops were princes and clergy clerked for royalty. Many of the second sons of the great families made fortunes in the Church. They made up the majority of the seats of hierarchy within the Church's structure. Corruption was widespread and reform was needed. Into this mix came a number of both baptized and clergy who read the Bible in a surprising, different way, though it would be naïve to assume that the Reformation they initiated was motivated purely by scripture. Other principalities were nipping at the heels of the Church, hungry for land, wealth, and power. The mix of religious fervor and Machiavellian opportunism made for a lethal cocktail that reshaped the Church more radically than at any time since the end of the fourth century.

By the time of the Reformation, church buildings and liturgy were no longer about people. The clergy had fetishized the act of Eucharistic consecration. People no longer participated in the liturgy; they were spectators.

The liturgy no longer emphasized hearing or responding. People were distant from liturgical action and the Eucharist was mysterious and unearthly. A high priesthood was in charge of the holy items.[2] The holy world was wholly separate from the real world, and a religious professional carefully and ritually prepared the heavenly banquet table.

Among the baptized, charismatic movements were afoot. Dissatisfaction with the Church caused people to seek meaning elsewhere. Nomadic prophets and preachers stirred up religious fervor among the laity. They preached against the government and the Church. Hans Boehm was one such preacher. He told villagers in Niclashausen in 1476 that "the whole country was mired in wantonness and, unless people were ready to do penance and change their wicked ways, god would let all Germany go to destruction."[3] The Renaissance had encouraged literacy among the laity, and the newly educated evinced a hunger for the scriptures and for new teachings. Their energy was harnessed for reform, and lay movements sprang up.[4]

This emphasis on lay ministry is obvious in the writings of the famous reformers. Martin Luther embraced the "priesthood of all believers," a crucial phrase in the lexicon of the reformed baptized.[5] Bible reading and personal piety animated the private lives of the baptized and were lived out in the public square. Personal piety planted the idea that one's personal faith was one choice among many other choices. One did not need to be Roman Catholic, but could be Protestant and, more specifically, a follower of Calvin, Luther, or Zwingli. This ability to choose resulted in some choices being right and some wrong, some righteous and some heretical. Sibling rivalry, the willingness to kill the other and its competition for souls, unleashed a blood bath orchestrated by Protestants and Catholics alike, with many caught in the middle.[6] And yet, for all this darkness, the reformers longed to undo the trappings of principality and return the Church to a nobler faith in Christ. Ironically, their efforts seemed to metastasize the institution, rather than kill it. The churchly principality became a multitude of churchly principalities.

There were many of these efforts to return the Church to a simpler faith and a mission that more closely resembled the mission of Christ. Embracing the divestment of power embodied in a vulnerable, crucified

Jesus was not part of their agenda, however. The Reformation was not a reign of peace. Violence and bloodshed plagued the *Pax Reformacione* because the reformers did not reject the idea of a Christian state. By pinning the downfall of the Church on the growth of papal power in the sixth century, the reformers were able to sidestep the question of whether a Constantinian Church could ever be truly faithful.[7] The reformers applied the great heresies as the touchpoints of their critique of the Church's structures: works righteousness (Pelagianism); the cults that worshiped saints instead of God directly (hagiolatry); and an economic model sustained by sacraments bought and paid for (sacramentalism). They were right in what was wrong. The reformers did not go far enough back in history, though, looking only to reform the church of the Middle Ages rather than returning to the earliest examples of the Jesus movement. The ecclesia, the church of Jesus, had not been seen on earth in a long time. The way of peace had been invisibly diffused within a web of imperial bureaucracy. In other words, the reformers misdiagnosed the roots of the problem and, instead of recreating the ancient calling of people into community, they recreated systems with similar issues around power and corruption. They may have in fact thrown aside some of the very best of the sacramental life in their house cleaning. Compounding the reformers' misdiagnosis was that many regarded all sacramental life as superstitious.[8]

The reformers also embraced secularism. They affirmed that God called people into professional vocations. Their rejection of the medieval economy accelerated the emergence of "a-religious" secular vocations. The state itself eventually became one of them. I do not think that the reformers intentionally sought to secularize the vocations. Making creation completely independent from the governance of Christ was not their goal. When we look at their correspondence and writings, we see that they thought they could control the powers of the state and politicians through instruction and good biblical argument. Furthermore, they were clear, as were the first Christians, that some professions were flat out unchristian. Those included monk, banker/lender, and prostitute. They appear to have been fine with monarch, paid soldiers, and those who carried out capital punishment. The Reformers were quickly outmaneuvered by the politicians and unmoored from the structure of the imperial Church as the autonomy of the state and secular vocations continued to develop, which ultimately set up religious belief in the state's right to reign as it chose.[9] Like Christians of the fourth century, the reformers translated the Empire into the divine providence of God. They marched everyone into modern secularism and individualism.[10] The theology of reformation declared princes and kingdoms embodied a kind of higher vocation of God and were duly appointed by God.[11]

The reformers' understanding of the state and its participation in divine providence unleashed religious warfare with the Roman Catholics in a new way. Christian states fought other Christian states. Christian sibling rivalry was outsourced to states and tribes. The work of Jesus no longer sat at the center of history, nor did the Church Universal. History was in the hands of the secular principalities and powers. The Church had become a member of the state—not the other way round. The ruler had all the powers, both earthly and heavenly. The Church continued to make the case that it held the power, but it was clear that it was subservient to the state. In the great Reformation cities (Zurich, Bern, and Geneva), the Church was a part of the administration of the government. The legal system applied reform principles. The Augustinian divide of the invisible and visible Church was taken as a given, in part, because the true Church could not be harmed by whatever the imperial or worldly church did. The reformers desired a complete renewal of society so that a more visible version of the invisible Church might be present in the world. However, the powers and principalities were greater and more uncontrollable once they were unbound from the Roman Church's control and structure.

Unleashing the drive toward autonomy in these other realms of culture had impacts far beyond politics. Ordinary vocations functioned independently of the Church in the same manner as princely ones. Classes and occupations became independent, divine callings with their own vocabularies, requirements, and communities. The reformers also freed scientific thought from the constraints of theology, making deism and atheism possible.[12] The forces the reformers unleashed in order to aid their struggles against Rome turned against them as well. The state claimed its own power. It no longer needed the Holy Roman Emperor to crown its rulers.

The acceptance of the necessity of the Empire in the fourth century was the first step. The development of modern secularism by the reformers in the fifteenth was the second.

The eighteenth through the twentieth centuries saw a growth in mission and a growth in lay participation in governance. Both ensured that the Church principality remained a strong, wealthy, and powerful institution. But over time, the Church slowly disconnected from the circles of power where it had held great authority up until the Reformation. From the time the Roman Pope first helped to raise an army to restore Rome after the fall of the Roman Empire until the eighteenth century, the Christian church had enjoyed a seat at the tables of power for more than a thousand years. In a relatively short amount of time, two hundred years, the Church was ushered out of such stations of power. By the middle of the twentieth century, the Church no longer had the clout it had once enjoyed and the ears of power were closed to its entreaties.

Colonization of the developing world was the context for the Church's expansion of mission. The English Church sent chaplains to care for settlers abroad, while the Spanish sent missionaries to convert the indigenous populations in the new lands. The Church continued to reckon with the violence of colonial missions, which included the theft of resources and the trafficking of humans. In the late nineteenth century churches sent missionaries out globally, literally taking Christianity to the ends of the world. It was a massive effort supported by the stewardship of the baptized. Roman Catholics and monastics were the first missionaries. By the middle of the twentieth century, Protestants had taken over the vast amount of missionary work.[13]

The demands of an expanded mission meant new churches needed to be built. From the country's emergence from the American Revolution, across westward expansion, and well into the twentieth century, Roman Catholics and Protestants built them in great numbers all across America. They built in varying styles, from basilicas to Gothic Revival. Secular traditions like functionalism and modernism impacted how these spaces were designed. American congregations tended to look eastward and mimic the churches of Europe. Great temples were constructed, like the National

Cathedral in Washington, DC, along with small churches in neighborhoods and rural communities. Liturgy in the Roman Catholic tradition
remained focused on the font, lectern, and altar. Various liturgical reforms
experimented with different seating arrangements to help reengage
people, but baptism, reading of scripture, and the Mass remained central. Meanwhile, Protestants continued to create spaces that emphasized
preaching and singing. The liturgy of the Word was the focal point.

How was this all possible? First, because of the creation of leisure time.
Industrialization created a surplus of time, and the Church filled it. Cities
established parks for the use of leisure time, spectator sports emerged as
a way to spend leisure time, and "childhood" was created out of the lux-
ury of leisure time. Local parishes were the center of people's leisure lives.
They promoted speakers, programs, and provided Christian education.
Prior to industrialization, less than 20 percent of members actually went
to church.[14] The Church also benefited from a lack of competition. There
were no Sunday sports for adults or youth. There was no massive communication or entertainment complexes to draw attention. Businesses were
closed on Sundays. Certain things could not be purchased on Sundays.
Churches grew furiously, especially in the United States. As populations
boomed after World War II, American churches boomed as well.

This truly American church movement needed new forms of financial
support. Out from under the established church of the colonies, American
Christianity would go through various stages regarding the funding of
church and mission alike. Immediately following the Revolution, congregations innovated new models of income generation as, for the first
time in centuries, Christian communities had to survive without government assistance. Pew rentals were a first means of addressing this problem. George Washington paid for a pew at Christ Church in Philadelphia,
St. Paul's Chapel in New York City, and Christ Church in Alexandria,
Virginia. Eventually, the pew rentals went away and congregations began
to set budgets and invite parishioners to pledge the funds needed for the
year. They would literally pass a book around to the heads of the families
and have them write their pledge in the book. By the nineteenth century,
many churches had a few members meeting and setting the budget with

the priest. This was still common in some congregations in this century. Then a plan emerged by which people would give each Sunday for a different need within the community. By the second half of the last century, pledge campaigns or stewardship drives were the modus operandi for fundraising among churches in the United States.

Clergy formation also underwent a radical transformation. After the Reformation, there was a drive to train more people in the skills of pastoring. Prospective clergy were taught to preach and care for the souls entrusted to their care. Well into the nineteenth century, most clergy serving in the fledgling country were still trained overseas. Growth in a desire to have locally trained clergy meant there was a need to create American seminaries. In 1808, the Massachusetts Congregationalists founded Andover Theological Seminary. Other denominations soon followed. Episcopalians founded General Seminary in New York in 1817, Virginia Theological Seminary in 1823, Yale Divinity School in 1854, and The Philadelphia Divinity School in 1857. These seminaries functioned quite differently from the earlier Bucer and Jesuit examples. Seminaries became professional schools preparing people for the care and feeding of a growing American Church. The models for theological study that we inherited are deeply rooted in these changes, and in the shifts that came about through innovations in science and critical study. When I went to seminary in the early 1990s, the curriculum was dependent on the innovations of theologian Friedrich Schleiermacher. He adapted a historical, critical, and philosophical approach to the study of Christian history, the Bible, and theology, with a strong pietistic flavor. He believed that Christianity was a way of feeling, knowing, and doing. Students were expected to master a scientific and critical approach to the corpus of Christian thought, while always keeping an eye on the practice of ministry in a community. Eventually classes were added that focused on pastoral care and parish administration, and Clinical Pastoral Education (using the hospital) became ubiquitous as an answer to the call from congregations and denominational structures to deal with changing forces on the ground. Licensing exams, like the Episcopal Church's own General Ordination Exams, were created. Seminaries intended to create a professional class of clergy who were specialists, well equipped for the work of mission. One of my professors, the Rev. Dr. Howard Hanchey, used to quip, "You are getting a Masters in Divinity. You will be a Master of the Divine." This mastery of churchy things amplified a growing divide between clergy and laity who were not masters of church things.

The twentieth century was the peak of the post-Reformation Church's size and self-confidence. Denominational churches focused on governance and standardization. They mimicked the style of modern corporations, emphasizing command and control, and centralizing the mechanisms of mission and ministry. The growth of program and administrative bureau-cracies were hallmarks of this period of organizational life. In the Episcopal Church, membership grew from 1.1 million members in 1925 to a peak of over 3.4 million members in the mid-1960s,[15] including the dioceses in the U.S. and a multinational mission field that stretched across the globe.

More recently, the Episcopal Church, like every large denomination, has decreased in numbers and programs, while not drastically reorganizing for the new mission context. Mainline churches have not acknowledged the evolving needs of the Church and the mission it serves. Clergy are swamped with organizational requirements that are artifacts of a bygone era. The hierarchy, structure, and governance that we modeled on cutting edge corporate practice is now over eighty years old and has become bur-densome. There is a growing disconnect between those who lead and the grassroots movements of lay mission and service. The Church remains mired in culture wars, wringing its hands over shrinking attendance, and trying to save itself by better budgeting in the wake of shrinking resources. The institutional Church of today struggles to sustain aging structures, repeatedly tries to force uniformity over unity, and desperately attempts to create diversity by legislation at conventions. The world has changed, and we are at a loss for how to respond.

CHAPTER EIGHT
A Misguided Strategy

I did set out to be holy and to be perfect exemplar and to fulfill all of my vows, baptismal and ordained, and we speak of ordination in the Episcopal Church as being set apart. It's part of the job. But I didn't want to be set apart anymore.

—Barbara Brown Taylor[1]

After sixteen hundred years of institutional growth, the principality and its vocations have been transformed from a movement into a power and authority. In the West, churches are struggling, which is to say that the Episcopal Church is not alone. Membership in the Episcopal Church has been dropping steadily since the 1980s. Losses have approximated 30 percent in fifteen years. Baptisms are down by half in that same time period. Marriages are down by 30 percent. Compared to other denominations, the Episcopal Church (TEC) is the biggest loser.[2] An interesting look at the totality of the Anglican Communion can be found in David Goodhew's *Growth and Decline in the Anglican Communion*.[3] The loss in numbers has affected how the Episcopal Church approaches vocation, and our approach to vocation has affected the church.

The ministry of the church has resembled a business for the last century. Most recent studies of vocation have focused on seminaries and how to save them. This focus is the result of our denominational assumption

that solving problems with the clergy would mean more robust enroll-
ment in seminaries, which would in turn reverse the numerical decline that
preoccupies us. Take, for example, the report to General Convention published in 1967, often referred to as the "Pusey Report," which is subtitled
"Ministry for Tomorrow." It was produced by a working group tasked with
assessing the present and future state of theological education within the
Episcopal Church. The chair of the committee was Nathan M. Pusey. The
assumptions that undergird this report and the questions it asks are fasci-
nating, given the present state of our church.

The Pusey Report[4] begins by asserting that ministry must always be
reconsidered in light of new contexts and historic shifts in culture. Leaning
on the work of H. Richard Niebuhr, the report traces a shift happening in
the United States, from an agrarian society to a more urban one. The report
also argues that scientific discoveries have placed pressure upon the work
of theology itself. The report references the work of Langdon Gilkey as it
pauses to consider the nature of "personal holiness" and the need to reclaim
the Samaritan work of loving neighbor.[5] The report also warns the church
about changing norms around "work and leisure," a growth in conflict,
and the "depersonalization" of society.[6] Rather than grappling with these
issues, the report takes a turn toward clericalism as it focuses on the "heri-
tage" of the church—meaning ministers and seminaries.[7] Any analysis of
the impact these shifts have on the whole community of the baptized is
suspiciously absent.

Even when the report is following a sound course, the true aim is to
shore up the ordained ministry. The report points out that we are to be a
community for the service of God. We are to be inspired for work—for
mission. The authors say, "'Being saved' does not mean self-congratulation
in a corner; it should mean going out to risk all in the service of one's
fellows beyond the church—and sometimes those in it."[8] Though these
inspirational words are directed at everyone, it is clear that the committee's
chief concern is clergy who can inspire such work. They quickly turn to the
"equipper," "interpreter," "reconciler and counselor," "pastor," and "celebra-
tor."[9] Only by reading between the lines of the report do we find glimpses
of ministry for the baptized, who are almost entirely missing from the

report. There is a brief mention that the seminaries should pay attention to the growing need for education for the baptized. The report calls the church's record on Christian education "lamentable."[10] The report fails to foresee how our seminaries have begun to devote much of their work to providing theological training for laypeople. The writers of the report seem not to believe that the baptized are essential to the mission of the church. The report also assumes changing strategy will address the cultural change the report identifies. The writers underestimated the economic shifts caused by urban migration and the increasing cost of running a church. I talk a bit about this in my earlier book, *Church*. Our organization is at the whim of very real socioeconomic forces.[11] Finally, absent from the report is any acknowledgement that we have too many seminaries—a statement often erroneously attributed to the report.

The report of the Episcopal Church's Board of Theological Education is also worth considering. The report deals with the problem of raising funds for seminary through the 1 percent Seminary Sunday plan. The writers were hopeful that their beta testing of online, computer-based education would bear some fruit. However, there has been very little success to show for these efforts and hopes.[12] The report makes the sobering statement that

> by the year 2015, the church must find successors for 5,000 (60%) of today's active clergy. What the church is turning toward in meeting this challenge is uncertain, but it has seemed to be turning away from its established seminaries.[13]

The report is rightly concerned about the cost of educating one clergyperson. It acknowledges that the seminaries are geographically distributed without thought to access for students. Cost, geographical location, and viability make the seminary experience difficult for all—especially those without resources or who come from different ethnic backgrounds.[14] The report offers this bleak outlook:

> The eleven Episcopal seminaries are small and many are growing smaller. Taken together, they contain only 155 full-time faculty who

serve 1100 students, 600 of whom are in the ordination track creating
a very low 7 to 1 student-faculty ratio, almost unmatched in higher
education. As separate institutions, they are continually challenged
to serve the mission of the church within the limitations imposed by
their small size and high fixed costs.[15]

The report notes the rise in the age of clergy, their lack of preparedness for
the complexities of ministry, and a diverse understanding of what clergy are
formed to accomplish.[16] As of the writing of this book, the report is twenty
years old. It signals that the Episcopal Church had begun to wake to the
changing reality of the higher education in the west, but it also reveals that
no deliberate actions have been taken. Today we sit at the end of a decade
of change in theological education marked by lower enrollments, closings,
mergers, and radical adaptations prompted neither by foresight or hindsight but instead by financial crisis. What is true for the Episcopal Church
is true across the landscape of theological education for all denominational
and nondenominational seminaries.

   We turn now to the 2015 Ministry Development Report to General
Convention, which was created by a commission that met between General
Conventions with a very specific goal: to help the General Convention and
the wider church enable the ministry of the baptized. The report states at
the outset that it will "recommend policies and strategies to the General
Convention for the formation, development and exercise of ministry by
all baptized persons (lay persons, bishops, priests, and deacons)."[17] This
is a great statement. It is clear, supportive, and invites curiosity about the
ministry of all the baptized. Then it quickly shifts and says that it intends
to "recommend strategies to General Convention for the development
and support of networks of individuals, diocesan Committees and commissions, agencies and institutions engaged in recruitment, gifts discernment, education and training for ministry, leadership development, and
deployment."[18] The true purpose of the report becomes obvious later on
as the writers pledge to "study the needs and trends of theological education for all baptized persons, including seminary education and life-long
learning, and recommend strategies to General Convention to strengthen

theological education for all baptized persons."[19] A cursory survey of fifty years of ministry reports reveal that talking about seminaries is the great black hole for all of these conversations.

The report ends up focusing on the task of raising up clergy with only a cursory mention of the baptized. We speak a lot about the ministry of the baptized, and what we mean by that is the work inside of the church building and the preparation of those who should go to seminary. It is disheartening to look through our denomination's attempts to talk about the "ministry of the baptized" and see over and over again a focus on how we get the baptized into seminary or the life support needed for our seminaries. In the last twenty years the Episcopal Church has innovated a new process for ordination within our canons called Title III. We have spent a lot of money tinkering with the work of Commission on Ministries. Meanwhile, the work of formation and discernment has been left to local rectors.

Before we conclude this chapter that has been dominated by our present era's clergy-centrism, I want to honor the fact that there has been an honest effort to assess the quality of lay education and formation within our church. Programs for Sunday morning and inquirers classes along with the church's teaching series have created a more unified approach to Christian formation at the local congregational level. Formation leaders have promoted "lifelong Christian formation" as a goal. They have dovetailed the work of formation with the five marks of mission. In 2012 an effort was made to insure funding for lifelong formation, but the money never materialized. Various other task forces and study groups have provided material that augments the work coming out of the Church Center. Church Publishing has tried to address the lack of material for Christian formation by including study questions in many of its newly published work. Parachurch organizations like Forward Movement, The Episcopal Church Foundation, and Forma have provided support for professional educators, consultants, and parish and diocesan church staff in search of quality formation materials. The Center for Theological Education at Virginia Seminary has a legacy of doing this work and is working even now to sort out new media forms and provide access to formation materials for the baptized.

Overall, I think the last sixty years of thinking about formation has been dominated by a search for a unified education plan for adults. Even the Pusey Report hoped for such a thing. The notion that there is one perfect formation tool has animated curricula authors and church formation people who seek a programmatic fix for what ails us. This period of church history has been in service to a particular pedagogy, where we give information to people. The season of local churches with clergy specialists educating the baptized may be a pedagogical trope whose time is past.

The Christian disciple today has access to a world wide web of materials. There is plenty out there for a curious new Christian to discover. Even the maturing disciple can find groups, Bible studies, and prayer materials to help them grow for the mission of Christ. The church remains stuck in the past, approaching the internet as an unreal space filled with individuals lacking community. The church is just now beginning to understand that there is much work to do if we are to engage in mission that is not limited to one worldly abode alone. The Episcopal Church's paper on evangelism, which includes online evangelism, is a good example of this new focus.

What is happening at seminaries signals the nature of our current crisis, if only we would pay attention. Seminary deans will tell you that students entering seminary twenty years ago had a greater understanding of what it meant to be an Episcopalian than those entering today. Much of their forming of first-year students is spent helping them understand exactly what an Episcopalian is. This might be considered the canary in the coal mine of adult spiritual formation. If a whole section of leaders whom we have raised up to take on the ministry of the sacraments are no longer carrying Episcopal DNA, then our past efforts to make a significant impact on adult formation across the church have failed. We could say the same for adults coming out of confirmation classes, or deputies to General Convention, or delegates to our diocesan councils and conventions. Our baptized members are ill-prepared to share in the ministries of the church because they have not been taught an Episcopal voice.

In the Episcopal Diocese of Texas, the Rev. Jane Patterson and the Rev. John Lewis have helped us rethink discernment. We agreed that the church has not focused much attention or resources on lay members of our churches. We have not helped them discern their vocations to ministry and mission in the wider world. At both the parish level and the diocesan level, we seldom teach Christian discernment as a spiritual tool and practice for daily living. The church itself has a wealth of resources on Christian discernment and vocation, yet we rarely share this wisdom with the baptized. We do not bring it to bear to help people—especially our younger adults—identify the various ways God is calling them to service in the world.

Into this mix has entered our Presiding Bishop Michael Curry, who has invited the church to join the "Jesus Movement." Curry says:

> God came among us in the person of Jesus of Nazareth to show us the Way. He came to show us the Way to life, the Way to love. He came to show us the Way beyond what often can be the nightmares of our own devising's and into the dream of God's intending. That's why, when Jesus called his first followers he did it with the simple words "Follow me." "Follow me," he said, "and I will make you fish for people." Follow me and love will show you how to become more than you ever dreamed you could be. Follow me and I will help you change the world from the nightmare it often is into the dream that God intends. Jesus came and started a movement and we are the Episcopal branch of the Jesus movement. . . .
>
> Now is our time to go—to go into the world to share the good news of God and Jesus Christ, to go into the world and help to be agents and instruments of God's reconciliation, to go into the world, let the world know that there is a God who loves us, a God who will not let us go, and that that love can set us all free.[20]

Curry's message is a clarion call that echoes the invitation of God described in our first chapters. It is a call that taps into the imagination of God and invites us to a different way of behaving. Too many will hear Curry telling them that we just need to work harder at what we are doing. Too many will believe that joining the Jesus Movement will require little transformation and pain. To become part of this Jesus Movement will require turning our institutional structures upside down—literally. It will demand that we become a lay-led, clergy-supported church. We will have to reject our tendency to be a clergy-led, lay-supported church. This call will require new types of formation, new types of discernment, and new types of training for mission.

The church suffers an infection called "theory-induced blindness."[21] We have accepted a theory that our current manner of formation tied to seminary education is the only tool for ministry preparation. We have equated seminary education with learning. Consequently, we are blind to the new tools at our disposal. At the end of the day, the church needs a variety of models for training. These models need to orient laypeople for mission. Seminaries who are training in old models, with old tools, behind self-imposed walls, and disconnected from the new mission context are preparing students for a church that is not going to exist much longer. Such seminaries are not necessary for formation in the future church. Those graduating from seminary today, trained in an old model of church, will impact church leadership for the next thirty years, which means we are already producing clergy with a clericalist model of ministry that will keep the church imprisoned through 2050. The question before us is, How will we create mutual ministry where people are no longer set apart, above, and beyond the work of the Jesus Movement?

CHAPTER NINE

Shalom Means Otherness

*Imitatio dei. Imitatio Christi. Imitation of God. Imitation of Christ is
God's dream for us. God's imagination for us.*

—Ellen Davis[1]

Today's Church is not the church that Jesus inaugurated as the
first fruits of the kingdom of peace. Nonetheless we are called to
work within the Church we have, renewing it for the purposes
Christ intended. The Church we have must do the work of the gospel:
being God's voice and partnering with God to create the kingdom of
shalom. We are to imitate God and Christ Jesus and be God's hands, feet,
and body in the world. Alcoholics Anonymous's famed Twelve Steps give
us three principles that are useful for the task of renewing the vocation of
the Church. First, the tools we used to get here may not help us get where
Jesus is pointing going forward. Second, we must identify what we can
change, what we cannot change, and know the difference between the
two. Third, we cannot keep doing the same thing over and over again and
expect different results. With an eye toward these three principles, let us
take a few steps toward a new understanding of vocation for the Church.

Moving in this new direction requires us to acknowledge that the
Church is overwhelmed with challenges. We no longer enjoy the favor of
secular empires. The Constantinian era is over. The codependency between
Church and state that he established centuries ago has fallen apart. In

truth, this codependency was not particularly good for God's mission, even when the imperial Church was at its best. Our expulsion from the halls of power should force us to change the way we think about our work as the Church. We cannot say, "The Age of Constantine is over," and continue working as though it endures. We no longer live in a Christian world. Theologian William Stringfellow wrote, "For a Christian, there is such a commitment as decent respect and open affection for the country of one's citizenship. But this is not the same as a patriotism which is idolatrous and deadly. A Christian gladly renders the former—it is what is due to Caesar in this world—but, by the virtue of Christ, that is *all* that belongs to Caesar."[2] Today the state is, at best, an absent and disinterested parent, or, at worst, a hostile power over and against God's community of shalom. As we wake up from our imperial dream and remove the blinders of institution, we are compelled to acknowledge that the progress of human history is not synonymous with God's providence. Our national history is not synonymous with God's providence. The imperial Church turned a blind eye to state-sanctioned violence and oppression, excusing such sin as the necessary working out of God's providence. In the West, we sold out God's mission for tacit approval of the state. This compromise has created divisions within our congregations because we have not converted our people to see that God has a completely different kind of kingdom to enact in this world and the next.

We must recover an awareness of our function as bearers of God's shalom. There are no external powers indebted to or responsible for this mission. We live in a world crossed by sibling rivalries, and the powers and authorities that enable these rivalries will labor to bring our aspirations down to their level. These powers will attempt to use the Church for their own purposes and not for God's. We must value the Church's vocation so highly that, when we are gazed upon, we appear visibly distinct from the world and its powers.[3] Our society has lots of work to do, and, we, as Christians, may have opinions about how such work should be accomplished, based on the gospel. Yet we must share with the early Church a mind that reunifies creation and properly places the narrative where it should be. We are not talking about our choices, sin, and brokenness that evade death by achieving a better life. We are instead proclaiming that God has, in the work of Jesus, completely flipped the conversation from life and death to death and resurrection. With this mind and perspective, then, we may enjoy what Stringfellow calls "decent respect and open affection for the country of one's citizenship."[4] However, that is different from the idolatry of the state that allows it to do violence in our name. We are freed from nurturing the powers of this world. We are freed to see that the state may in fact have some organizational work that is needed and in need of our support. We can even cooperate with the state on social reform and supporting programs that support human flourishing. But we will remain aware that the state is still Caesar and affection may be given, but that is all it will receive. We are citizens of a different reign with different values and a different story. We are members of the reign of shalom. Human flourishing and peace cannot be supported by the Church if they come at the expense of human life or are secured by violence; those are the ways of this world. To follow those ways is to partner with the imposters of God.[5]

Reconnecting our mission to a theology of the Cross firmly planted on the dung heap of the world will erode our attachment to a history of collusion with principalities. Such a Church could acknowledge that the world is chaotic, and yet rejoice that the powers fomenting this chaos have no power over us, because nothing can separate us from God and God's love. No powers and authorities tell us who is in and who is out.[6] To live under the banner of the Cross means the baptized are citizens of God's kingdom before anything else. We define ourselves by these words from the 1979 Book of Common Prayer: "Jesus Christ our Lord you have received us as your sons and daughters, made us citizens of your kingdom, and given us the Holy Spirit to guide us into all truth."[7] We accept the reality that there is no secular world; there is only God's creation. To be such a Church, we must begin breaking down the Constantinian and Reformation walls. There is no world separate from God's creation, none that is free from the lordship of Christ. All community, including the community of Christ— the Church—is under his benevolent lordship, and is to be judged by his benevolence on the Last Day.

The Church that accepts the Constantinian and Reformation world-view will always be at odds with the Lordship of Christ and the reign of peace. The Constantinian church and its empire were inept at bringing about God's community of shalom with Christ at its head. While in good faith the Church attempted to deal with the incompatibility by developing the theology of the invisible church, it had the end effect of raising secular autonomy. Our survey of history reveals the decay of God's mission within the church principality: a slow, ironic "de-Christianizing" of the West fully supported by the Church itself.[8] The world lacks meaning without Christ. Creation's, and humanity's, only dignity is given by Christ and Christ's mission of peace.

We must reject the claim that the accumulation of material comforts and the freedoms of a secular society represent the end of history. We will also have to set aside our state citizenship. Instead, we must declare that the community of peace inaugurated by Christ includes every tribe, nation, tongue, and people.[9] The divisions in the future Church will be between those who desire the reign of peace and those who defend the concealed religion of secularism. The present-day war between liberal and conservative faith are really two sides of the same reformed coin. What is truly at stake is not a moral game, but instead the vocation of the Church as an agent of God's visible kingdom of peace. The Church that emerges by reengaging its vocation of shalom will not reduce the kingdom of God to a spiritualized adornment of the self, a hobby, or accept the Church's place as just another principality. It will approach the world and its institutions, including the Church, with great care, acknowledging the ways that these institutions are in direct conflict with Christ's reign of shalom.

The vocation of the Church is a universal call by God. The invitation to peace is a universal invitation. This catholic invitation is not the reformer's idea that the few chosen are to live into a demanding life, fail, and be for-given and then go on living the unrealized life of peace. When the Church treats the baptized this way, it builds into the system the secret conviction that God's mission is not a rule that can be lived out, but is a nice thought that is unrealistic in practice. This is the road traveled by the reformers and puritans. Another way the Church dismisses its vocation is the pretense that Christ's vision was of an invisible world that everyone can live into, so active repentance and conversion are not required. This is the pre-Reformation world. The truth is God's call to peace is universal and can be accomplished in this world and the next. God actually expects humanity to put down its weapons and divest itself of the self-centeredness that drives sibling rivalry. Both ways of shirking God's call described above are driven by the Church's failure to convert the powers in opposition to God.

The vocation of the Church will also be to remind itself that there is authentic work in the world that is at odds with the values associated with God's kingdom of peace. This is a hard conversation to have. For fear of numerical decline, we have not spoken the truth to our members, acknowledging that some professions compromise our capacity to spread shalom in the world. It is worth acknowledging that the early Church deemed many professions as being completely off-limits to the baptized. Although it may be difficult and even unwise to make such pronouncements in our current context, we cannot endorse the false claim that violence is ever appropriate for the Christian, even when necessitated by the state. For instance, we have plenty of soldiers, police officers, and prison guards in our pews. We must help them to deal with their work by directly confronting the religious predicament they may find themselves in from time to time.[10] It is as if we are asking the same questions we have asked and failed to answer for over a millennium. The Constantinian formularies of church and state do not work. There is no making church great again. Going back and attempting the same arguments developed by the empirical church is to try the same thing over and over again hoping for different results. This, of course, is the definition of insanity. We must help people come to terms with how their work might be at odds with God's shalom and not withdraw from difficult conversations. Employment that is violent and potentially involves the killing of others is not Christian work. Our dishonesty about this has contributed to the great psychological dissonance that infects our society. People who are compelled to harm others in the line of duty know that such duties are not the way of God. The mission of God in Christ rejects violence. Early Christians understood this as one of the reasons that the kingdom of Christ is categorically different from the world.[11]

The Church calls ordinary people to go in God's name. The Church invites people to be a blessing of peace for the whole world. With the words of shalom, the disciples and apostles of God in Christ Jesus speak on God's behalf, in word and action, into the wider community in which they find themselves. The Church understands that the community of peace, where diverse human interconnectivity is present, is where God does mighty works. These works are not violent. God does not sanction violence done in God's name. When the Church embraces its peaceful vocation given by God, it impacts our economic practices, our treatment of others, and our approach to formation. We continue to try and outsmart the cultural trends through effective and better programming. We will truly engage the gospel when we chose solidarity with the people of the world in which we find ourselves. This is the sacrificial foolishness of the Cross. The real church is one freed from performance in favor of one that gives itself over to the world God loved in which Christ became incarnate.

We must come to terms with our mission as a community of shalom. To embrace our calling, we have to acknowledge that our connection, our enmeshment, with a violent society is real. We spend our energy sanctimoniously marching around, waving a fist at the violent world outside our churches, but we do not deal honestly with our own people who participate in violent professions. Such hypocrisy generates tremendous conflict in our hearts and for our mission. Denominational churches have for a long time played the role of the national church. We have sanctioned the empire-building ambitions of the United States. We have been at war, and committing violent atrocities in the name of peace for 222 out of 239 years of our country's existence. *Pax Americana* is not peace. But the *Pax Americana* is deeply entangled with religion, with the divine right myth that poured holy water on our imperial ambitions. Our culture is a powerful mix of politics and religion grounded on the claim that the United States is God's city on a hill. But instruments of God's peace rarely succeed in empire building. The community that wishes to follow the Jesus of the Gospels and take on God's mission of peace will have to sort out the pastoral and political conflicts such a mission creates.

Jesus also intends for the Church to transform economies by its alternative way of sharing. In God's creation there is enough for everyone to have food to eat, clothes, shelter, and to engage in a vocation that has dignity. Because of its many and varied resources, endowments, and foundations, the Church must engage with the evils of capitalism. When we look back, we can see, in hindsight, our complicity in the crimes of colonialism, slavery, and genocide. We have not yet repented for our part in the system of dominion that is capitalism. For instance, in his encyclical letter *Centesimus Annus*, John Paul II gave a nod to the merits of free enterprise, private initiative, and profit but is cautious:

> It would appear that, on the level of individual nations and of international relations, the free market is the most efficient instrument for utilizing resources and effectively responding to needs. But this is true only for those needs which are "solvent," insofar as they are endowed with purchasing power, and for those resources which are "marketable," insofar as they are capable of obtaining a satisfactory price. But there are many human needs which find no place on the market. It is a strict duty of justice and truth not to allow fundamental human needs to remain unsatisfied and not to allow those burdened by such needs to perish.[12]

John Paul II cautioned us with these words following the collapse of Marxism:

> The Marxist solution has failed, but the realities of marginalization and exploitation remain in the world, especially the Third World, as does the reality of human alienation, especially in the more advanced countries. Against these phenomena the Church strongly raises her voice. Vast multitudes are still living in conditions of great material and moral poverty. The collapse of the Communist system in so many countries certainly removes an obstacle to facing these problems in an appropriate and realistic way, but it is not enough to bring about their solution. Indeed, there is a risk that a radical capitalistic ideology

could spread which refuses even to consider these problems, in the
a priori belief that any attempt to solve them is doomed to failure
and which blindly entrusts their solution to the free development of
market forces.[13]

To reengage the mission of peace, the Church, which is to be a different
kind of principality with a different kind of economy, will have to ponder
how it uses its wealth. Neither Marxism nor a benighted neoagrarian-
ism is an actionable solution. The Church is not responsible for choosing
economic systems for entire countries. Our problem is more local to us.
We need to think about the wealth of the Church, and the wealth of our
members, and how our assets are tied into a system that is based upon
imaginary wealth. Author, environmentalist, and cultural critic Wendell
Berry has much to say about the imaginary foundations of late capitalism.
I have been reading him since I first was introduced to his Port William
series that included the book *Jayber Crow*. Berry believes the core issue in
our present capitalist economy is that banks are selling "a bet on a debt as
an asset."[14] It is an economy based upon nonreal assets, set by and for a few
over the corporate good of the whole. I find Berry helpful here because he
writes about small-scale household economies. The word for economics
literally comes from the word *oikonomia*, meaning "household management." Economics have been part of the Church's mission from the very
beginning. There was a purse. Needed items were purchased for the support of the mission. Money was raised and redistributed to the poor and
those in need. Shelter, food, and protection were provided by the wider
community. Paul's letters testify that there was mission money raised to
fund missionary travel. Money was also raised to help with other community expenses. Moreover, we know that from the beginning certain
presbyters called bishops had the unique task of overseeing the purse. Up
until the fourth century, the collecting and funding of the work is pretty
forthright. Household management—economics—has always been part
of the Christian community.

Berry reminds us that household management is an integral part of
life. Herman Daly, an economist and professor of public policy writes,

"Oikonomia is the science or art of efficiently producing, distributing, and maintaining concrete use values for the household and community."[15] But our society has long since ceased to concern itself with household management. Our economics are a form of chrematistics, which is "the art of maximizing the accumulation by individuals of abstract exchange value in the form of money in the short run. Although our word 'economics' is derived from *oikonomia*, its present meaning is much closer to chrematistics."[16] "Chrematists" are invested in creating need, driving consumption, and growing the economy.[17] "Our economy," Berry notes, "has become an anti-economy, a financial system without a sound economic basis and without economic virtues."[18] Berry points to a different kind of economy based on creation and basic human need. In other words, Berry is proposing a virtuous economy that upends the nonvirtuous chrematistics of late capitalism.

Berry's economic vision dovetails with the reign of shalom. I offer it as a basis for how the Church manages its household in a world obsessed with chrematistics. Berry offers a few principles for what he calls the Great Economy, beginning in the same place the Church does: with everything. God's creation is the foundation; everything is included. Everything is connected and the parts participate and reflect the whole.[19] It includes humans, but humans are a part of the whole, like all other creatures. It is so expansive that we must create "little economies" for smaller communities. Our systems of exchange cannot diminish creation, humanity, or impinge upon the peaceableness of households. Therefore, Berry suggests there must be a "law of return." Such a law would cut against the terminal greed that plagues our chrematistic economy, making the virtues of "temperance" or "thrift" impossible. Berry's law of return forces us to acknowledge that the created order has finite boundaries. There is no limitless capacity for consumption.[20] Berry writes, "The industrial economy is based on invasion and pillage of the Great Economy."[21]

Only a community can help care for God's "Great Economy"—creation. Our chrematistic economy siloes us in our greed and consumption. Our vocations are construed competitively, and we are disabled from cooperating in the stewardship of creation. Competition among members of society becomes an object of devotion—a common societal virtue—and the common good is sacrificed for the benefit of a few. Berry says "economics has become the justifier and explainer of all the affairs of our daily life," competition has been "enshrined as the sovereign principle and ideal."[22] In other words, chrematistics with its unfettered capitalistic greed inhibits us from partnering with God and with one another in the Garden.

We must acknowledge that participating in the exchanges of late capitalism impoverishes our mission. Greed and the drive to consume and compete disrupt the household economy of shalom. The Church must function differently, within late capitalism, with a spiritual clarity and systems of exchange that are radically foreign to the world around us. We are all participants in late capitalism. There is no point in scapegoating here. Everyone who attends church participates in these systems of exchange in one way or another.

At the local level, Berry's critique challenges congregations and missional communities to make decisions about their footprints, both ecologically and economically. We have to see that these two things are connected. Congregations need to think about getting off the grid by consuming less energy. Congregations need to confront the likelihood that they have more building than they need. But so do larger Church bodies like dioceses and provinces and denominations. There is something inherently wrong with organizations that see the need for change in global ecological trends regarding fuel consumption but do not adjust their own consumption of energy and fuel for the massive meetings of thousands of people that they host. Similarly, dioceses need to consider how much money they spend to travel in cars. Local congregations could buy electricity together from green providers, but rivalry among local congregations tends to inhibit such collaboration. To be a peace-making community, the Church will have to come to terms with our own sins against the natural world. Our proclamation of God's reign of peace will not make sense until we reform our own violent practices of consumption.

The Church also needs to think about its endowments and foundations. They are immersed in the chrematistic economy. Yes, the investments we make are for doing good, but is the Church damaging its mission of peace by engaging in economic structures that create wealth for powers and principalities while disempowering the poor? The investment community is just now beginning to address this enmeshment between investment and the chrematistic economy. The Ford Foundation, helmed by globally recognized investor Peter Nadosy, is leading the way by committing up to $1 billion of its $12 billion endowment over the next ten years to the nascent investment field known as mission-related investing.[23] Nadosy and his team are doing a deep dive into projects that benefit the wider society along Ford's values. This is the future for Church investing. At the Episcopal Health Foundation (EHF), which has a $1.3 billion endowment, we have a goal to join Nadosy and the Ford Foundation by investing in people, health, and community. We hope to reform the foundations held and managed by the diocese along these lines. The impact of this work will not be obvious for years, but as a Church we believe that mission-related investing is the business of the shalom community.

The Episcopal Church has a huge amount of wealth that comes under the laws of the secular society for its management and use. This governance will test the Church by requiring certain measures be taken to safeguard the individual donor's requisitions. Just as other nonprofits are coming under greater public scrutiny of their investment strategy and their spending, so will the Church. Being a church will no longer provide protection from indiscriminate spending. More and more, I predict, the state will have oversight of how we spend our funds as just another nonprofit, church principality or not.

We also need to take a hard look at clergy compensation. Work, for ordained people, is diversifying as economic and cultural pressures limit the congregations' ability to maintain full-time clergy stipends. There is an actual increase in the cost of having full-time clergy. There is also an increase in the cost of electricity, water, and trash collection. Maintenance costs rise on older buildings. The trend in attendance is down for denominational and nondenominational churches alike. This makes for a toxic mix. Some congregations have hired bivocational clergy, who receive very little stipend, if any, and make their living at other jobs. Their role is

limited to being a sacramentalist and pastor. Bivocational clergy are often
trained through an alternative program because their employment prohib-
its them from spending three years in seminary. Other congregations pay
their clergy part-time. These jobs attract seminary-trained clergy who do
not require a full-time salary, perhaps because their spouses are the main
income earner in their household. And then there are the full-time paid
clergy. The vast majority of these are seminary trained. There are in fact
fewer of these today, with statistics indicating they make up about half of
the total pool of clergy.

The smaller number of full-time positions and the smaller number
of clergy mean that there is a market of demand. Moreover, within this
market of demand is a scale of complexity. Not all clergy can handle larger
congregations, which means that congregations pay for the best clergy
they can. This is very important to the system. It allows for judicatory leaders to build in salary equality for men, women, and to ensure clergy from
the LGBTQ community receive fair employment based upon the size,
context, and complexity of the congregation. Where clergy compensation
is capped at a flat rate, a number of problems emerge:

1. There is a huge gap between salaries of male clergy and women;
2. complex organizations within the system have a difficult time
   attracting the best talent within the system;
3. the system overall has a difficult time attracting new clergy with
   leadership skills because of salaries;
4. taking money and funding small churches undermines leadership
   and mission and does not bring growth.

Conversely, when congregations and diocesan leadership work together to
set compensation numbers we see the following:

1. Church leadership improves;
2. complex systems are able to attract better leaders using higher salaries and benefits;
3. and nonwhite male clergy tend to have better salaries in a system
   where the diocese and parish use salary comparisons.

I predict two coming issues of conflict within the American church. The first is that the growing number of small congregations will push to have their full-time clergy underwritten by the dwindling number of wealthy congregations. This will be a mistake. The second is that the Church, out of an excess of zeal, will attempt to cap clergy salaries at an arbitrary amount. This too will be bad for recruitment, deployment, and the long-term health of the Church.

Yet Berry's image of economics as household management challenges us. As we examine the issue of clergy pensions and compensation, the Church will have to work in a very precarious socioeconomic environment. I have a friend who pastors a church of three hundred and fifty people with a one million dollar budget. He did the numbers. The rising cost of maintenance, of clergy, of lay employees, of utilities means they are between one and two decades away from being led by a bivocational priest. The Church will have to figure out how to deal with the gap between professional clergy and those who are tentmaker clergy like Paul. As we navigate these present challenges and the many more that await us, we do so with faith. Our work is not to solve the many issues that confront us but rather to navigate them with courage, integrity, and trust under the banner of the Cross in such a manner that we are visibly distinct from the world and its powers. Above all, we must identify what we can change, accept what we cannot change, and seek God's wisdom to know the difference between the two.

CHAPTER TEN

Humans, Tools, and Commons

Whatever structurally does not fit the logic of machines is effectively filtered from a culture dominated by their use.

—Ivan Illich[1]

Our critique of the post-Constantinian Church has demonstrated how vocations have been compromised by both chrematistic valuation and complicity with secular power. But there is still more to say about the impact of our shifting economic practices. Our global economy has obliterated local communities, rendering them insufficient to meet their own needs, and making the people who live in them terminally isolated. The vast majority of human beings do not make anything, let alone make anything for themselves. Berry writes, "'Outsourcing' the manufacture of frivolities is at least partly frivolous; outsourcing the manufacture of necessities is entirely foolish."[2] Household economics must reclaim a local focus. "Neighborhoods" and "neighborliness" must remerge as important values. A yearning for neighbors is baked into the small batch movement, which is reconnecting producers and consumers, and individuals with the creative minds behind the products they purchase.[3] The small batch trend is bringing about local production of foods and household goods—many created inside homes and garages. Small batch bread, bourbon, clothing, and the farm-to-table movement are sacramental views of this trend in neighborliness.

The gospel community can further undermine the dehumanizing practice of the global market by focusing locally and adding value to the neighborhoods where their communities are embedded. The Church must partner with others and help people in local communities to relearn the art of household management, which has been obliterated from cradle to grave because chrematistic patterns of exchange have adhered to every part of life. The Church must help individuals remember themselves as parts of a family, because families are the foundation for rebuilding local communities. Jesus went to families. He met in homes. Family is the core of the shalom community. Chrematistic rituals of exchange wear away family bonds and even collapse friendship circles by the weight of the powerful, urgent drive to accumulate money. Rowan Williams, former archbishop of Canterbury, spoke to a group of economists about the emerging issues that an unencumbered system of competition has on individuals, their families, and their children. He said:

> An atmosphere of anxious and driven adult lives, a casual attitude to adult relationships, and the ways in which some employers continue to reward family-hostile patterns of working will all continue to create more confused, emotionally vulnerable or deprived young people. If we're looking for new criteria for economic decisions, we might start here and ask about the impact of any such decision on family life and the welfare of the young.[4]

Williams also points out that the human creature is meant for creativity. We have already spoken about God's invitation to be a partner. But chrematistic systems of exchange force people to live without space for imagination. Imaginative play is how we learn to question, to problem-solve, and to see the world with its future differently. Adults need space and time for play as much as children do.

> It is the extra things that make us human; simply meeting what we think are our material needs, making a living, is not uniquely human, just a more complicated version of ants in the anthill. One of the greatest legacies of the British labour movement has been a real

commitment to this—to the enlarging of minds and feelings (anyone who's been able to see that wonderful play, *The Pitmen Painters*, will know what I mean). So the question is how far economic decisions help or hinder a world in which that space for *thinking things might be different* is kept open.[5]

In Philip K. Dick's classic sci-fi novel entitled, *Do Androids Dream of Electric Sheep?*, later made into the popular film *Blade Runner*, androids can only mimic empathy but cannot truly express it. For Dick, empathic connection is the exclusive purview of human being. Nurturing family and friendship circles through play and a leisurely sharing of life and time expand the human capacity for understanding, sympathy, and empathy. Chrematistic systems of exchange demand that life be oriented around work. Self-interest and success are promoted in the workplace. Williams points out that such a culture "encourages you to struggle for your own individual interest and success, you are being encouraged to ignore the reality of other points of view—ultimately, to ignore the cost or the pain of others. The result may be a world where people are very articulate about their own feelings and pretty illiterate about how they impact on or appear to others—a world of which 'reality television' gives us some alarming glimpses."[6] We generally scapegoat individuals who demonstrate villainous lacks of empathy without looking at the social determinants that make such toxicity possible.

The Church as a community of shalom has much work to do in a world dominated by chrematistic exchange. Christian charity pushes us to reach out to the casualties of society, and the number of broken people continues to mount. The community of shalom is a different kind of life where families are celebrated, new families are formed, and all these families bless one another. People recover the value of the Sabbath. They discover that they are made for partnership with God and that imagination, play, and discovery rejuvenate human relationship. Such a community of shalom names the lie that things and people can only delight us if we have them in large quantities. To actually die with the most toys (a bumper sticker popular in the West) is to die with nothing. God comes as mystery, inviting human participation in a great narrative, which stands in stark contrast to the world where relationships, friendships, and families can only be known as commodities.[7] Williams points out that "an economic climate based on nothing but calculations of self-interest, sometimes fed by an amazingly distorted version of Darwinism, doesn't build a habitat for human beings; at best it builds a sort of fortified boxroom for paranoiacs (with full electronic services, of course)."[8] The modern Church has failed at grafting a theology of charity into the dominant culture of chrematistic exchange. The inverse has happened: chrematistic exchange has grafted itself into the heart of the Church. We have made the baptized and the clergy into commodities for the maintenance and support of the institution.

A renewed gathering of the followers of Jesus must break into the world, and break up the world. The gathering where bread is broken, stories shared, and prayers are offered reminds the local community that they are implicated in a narrative of peace. Such a renewed gathering also breaks up the constant work expected by chrematistic institutions. The gathering in God's name to proclaim the message of grace, reminding each other that all are invited into partnership with God, and giving thanks for a creation that has enough for all is an act of defiance in the face of chrematistic institutions promoting works righteousness, limited success for only the most devoted apostles, and a philosophy of private ownership and scarcity. In his book *Political Worship* Bernd Wannenwetsch observes:

> Worship again and again interrupts the course of the world. Through worship the Christian community testifies that the world is not its own. And this means also that it is not kept alive by politics, as the business of politics, which knows no sabbath, would have us believe. That is why the celebration of worship is not directed simply against this or that totalitarian regime; it is directed against the totalization of political existence in general.[9]

Christian community is one of the few ways that people can successfully resist the colonization of our bodies by the institutions of chrematistic exchange. We are slowly reverting to a model of social and political life where, through technology, the powers and authorities have a total claim on the body of every human being. Humans, once again, are seen as resources rather than beings.[10] The gathered community of shalom reveals this total control to be a lie. The human body is meant for a different end altogether. Gathering reminds the community of our heavenly purpose. Worship reminds the community of our heavenly purpose. In fact, the true beneficiaries of Easter are those who have suffered and died at the hands of unjust powers and institutions of chrematistic exchange for not even institutions as powerful as these can separate God from the faithful (Rom. 8:37–39). Christians remember the dead when we gather because our remembrance is a sign of our hope, and a declaration that the powers of death will have no victory.[11]

Sunday morning worship services are being changed as people make new communities that share meals in other settings. Certainly the missional movement and the farm-to-table gatherings of Christians are whittling away at the traditions we have received through the institutional Church. Borrowed spaces, public and private, are reshaping assumptions about what is needed for gathering. Jesus said that "something greater than temple is here" (Matt. 12:6). Jesus broke open the centralized faith of his day and redistributed the faith of his forbearers. For instance, Jesus used the term *worship* in only a few instances.[12] Worship is indeed part of what Christians do. We continue the notion of giving thanks to God, prayers, and worship that we received from our faith ancestors in the Mosaic or Sinai tradition. But Christians are doing more than simply worshiping God. The very act of gathering in relationship and holding hands resists commodification of our bodies.[13]

Another basic tool the shalom community uses to resist colonization is the *chabûrah*—the feast of friends. Neighborliness, as Peter Block, civic engineer and author, argues, is rooted in friendship. The community has an opportunity to engage in friendship with its surroundings. It bears witness to Jesus's willingness to eat and drink with others by engaging relationally with the community around him. "Service can be commoditized, friendship cannot."[14] The missional movement across the Church is rooted in this principle of friendship. This kind of friendship leads beyond outreach and the dehumanizing practices of toxic charity into a relationship of collaboration. It breaks open our inherited models of Christian community and knocks down the walls that buffer our private spaces. Friends are not bound by private space or false ideas of secular and sacred, but by agape: friendship love. As Wendell Berry writes, "A community is the mental and spiritual condition of knowing that the place is shared, and that the people who share the place define and limit the possibilities of each other's lives. It is the knowledge that people have of each other, their concern for each other, their trust in each other, the freedom with which they come and go among themselves."[15] He reminds us that the abdication of communal authority to the powers and authorities through governmental systems has freed us from each other in a toxic way. Reclaiming neighborliness as part of the communal life is essential to Christ's vision. No person can live unto themselves. It is simply impossible. But, more importantly, the personalization of neighborliness returns authority to the members of the small community the local church serves. Its members start to care for one another again, which taps into the inclusive DNA of the Jesus Movement.

A shalom community engaging in friendly partnership with its neighbors will gravitate toward the urgent issues that preoccupy the local community. If people in our neighborhood care about safe public spaces, transportation, economic development, crime, or education, then God cares about these things, as does the community of shalom in a living partnership with the neighborhood will invest in local remedies to all of these issues. It will invest in economic development and partnerships that empower those in need of a better life. Along with the financial investment and time investment, a community of peace will focus on raising up new leaders within their neighborhoods. Indigenous leadership or contextual leadership is essential for the success of such partnerships. This is how friendship works. Friends empower each other to share their voices and do things they did not think were possible. A Church resisting colonization will be busy helping its neighbors invest in each other so that cycles of violence are broken and a new vision of life together in peace becomes possible. Gathering for worship and service bears a visible public witness against the powers of this world, and undermines them by resetting the boundaries of physical space in the world.

Finally, a community of shalom will resist the powers of chrematistic exchange by recovering a commons that can be enjoyed by every member of a neighborhood. The privatization of land as resources, the eventual carving out of mineral rights, or eminent domain has contributed to our isolation by placing new boundaries upon our shared space. We view space as a commodity we individuals have the right to exploit rather than as part of a created order in which we all live and are invited to be partners together with God in managing (Gen. 1:26). The transformation of our lived environment from a space held in common to a series of spaces held privately serves the interests of the few while impoverishing the many. This has amounted to a slow appropriation of the "commons." Historically, the *commons* in the West, or the word *iriai* in the East, has designated the environment in which people lived. The commons were governed by custom and were characterized by shared access.[16] Ivan Illich explains:

> People called commons that part of the environment which lay beyond their own thresholds and outside of their own possessions, to which, however, they had recognized claims of usage, not to produce commodities but to provide for the subsistence of their households.[17]

The openness of the commons meant that people could fish, hunt, graze, collect wood, or plants.

> An oak tree might be in the commons. Its shade, in summer, is reserved for the shepherd and his flock; its acorns are reserved for the pigs of the neighboring peasants; its dry branches serve as fuel for the widows of the village; some of its fresh twigs in springtime are cut as ornaments for the church—and at sunset it might be the place for the village assembly.[18]

The use of the commons had limitations for the sake of sustainability, but the commons were shared spaces that made gathering with neighbors essential for individual life. The Church's position toward the practice of maintaining commons in cities and villages began to change in the fourth century. As became normative in Western society, the Church became a private property owner. Somehow the Church must reclaim its critique against the evacuation of the commons. Privatization of common resources inevitably leads to those resources becoming assets that undergird invisible wealth. This is the slippery slope of chrematistic exchange.

> Enclosure, once accepted, redefines community. Enclosure under-mines the local autonomy of community. Enclosure of the commons is thus as much in the interest of professionals and of state bureaucrats as it is in the interest of capitalists. Enclosure allows the bureaucrats to define local community as impotent to provide for its own survival.[19]

Enclosure of the commons allows for a sort of economic independence upon the enclosed resources and the commodities produced there. Conversely, people become tied to the land in a way that they were not prior to shared commons.

Furthermore, enclosed commons accentuate the separation of the secular and the sacred. The Church can take steps toward eroding private space by stepping across the lines that demarcate such enclosures. First, the Church can become a commons itself, gathering the local community, and sharing its resources for the improvement of the neighborhood. Second, the Church can offer the Eucharist in public and other private spaces. In this way, the gathering of people for *chabûrah*, the feast of friends, redefines the space. Both of these tools (worship and service) reinterpret the bound-aries of church space and reengage neighborhoods across the boundaries of private space. The Church's reentrance into public environs of any kind is a direct confrontation with the powers and the making of a feast there undermines the stories of scarcity, the survivalist mentality, and expands the political boundaries of acceptance.

CHAPTER ELEVEN

Professionalism and Deschooling Seminary

As the shape of Christianity changes and our churches adapt to a new world, we have a choice: we can drive our hearses around bemoaning every augur of death, or we can trust that the same God who raised Jesus from the dead is busy making something new. As long as Christians are breaking the bread and pouring the wine, as long as we are annointing the sick and baptizing sinners, as long as we are preaching the Word and paying attention, the church lives, and Jesus said even the gates of hell cannot prevail against it. We might as well trust him, since he knows a thing or two about the way out of the grave.

—Rachel Held Evans[1]

Over the years, the vocations of the Church have taken on the trappings of middle-class professions. Seminary training did not become common until after the Reformation. Before that, any training was reserved for those who managed the Church's vast organization, dealing with things like discipline, ordinations, and finances. Following the Reformation, general ordination training became normative. It is important to pull at this string in order to understand the challenge confronting the Church as we strive to imitate the mission community of Christ.

The professionalization of the clergy is one of the ways that the Church has colluded with chrematistic systems of exchange and turned people into commodities. This commodification is underwritten by our societal obsession with specialization. People live in professional siloes and no longer experience themselves as part of society as a diverse whole. In fact, the whole is completely occluded from view by our various siloes of professional culture. Specialization has unleashed an extraordinary flood of special knowledge, at the expense of the community itself. Wendell Berry writes, "Specialization is thus seen to be a way of institutionalizing, justifying, and paying highly for a calamitous disintegration and scattering-out of the various functions of character: workmanship, care, conscience, responsibility."[2] Siloed professionals live and die by the singular relevance of their particular product. Modernity has funneled all the transcendent energy generated by human life into the realm of the specialist. Professionals are solely responsible for perfecting themselves and bettering their specialty. They have no accountability to the wider community, and very little usefulness within the community.

Berry also argues that professionalism is a kind of estrangement. To be formed into one of modernity's vocational siloes is to be lifted out of one community and dropped into another. Specialists are dislocated. Such dislocations undermine the integrity of our local communities, and limit people's ability to acknowledge their mutual dependence. The healthiest communities have a sense of the whole baked into every part. Healthy communities are not composed of short-timers, employed for their special skills.[3]

Ivan Illich argues that professionalism creates needs within the community that are not necessary for the health and well-being of the community. The fragmentation of the body into specialties means that one person needs a multitude of specialists to complete basic tasks.[4] As professionals specialize by deconstructing their area of expertise, more professionals are required. This has an economic effect. The evolution from craftsman to professional has impacted the law itself.

By not taking the craftsman's counsel, you were a fool. For not taking liberal counsel, you were a masochist. Now the heavy arm of the law may reach out when you escape from the care that your surgeon or shrink have decided for you. From the merchant-craftsman or learned adviser, the professional has mutated into a crusading and commandeering philanthropist.[5] Our economy of chrematistic exchange creates a need for professionals, in exactly the same way that it makes us investors and consumers. Specialists tell you how to navigate the marketplace of ideas and things.

Professionals are secular theologians, arbiters of what is good for society, and what is good is defined as the bottom line. Incumbent in this system is a rejection of local value and relational value. There can be no debt forgiveness or bartering for goods and services. The professional is a priest who offers necessary services—"a crusading helper."[6] Moreover, the professional outlaws the "unorthodox" and "imposes solutions" on the system. They are the authority on advice, instruction, and direction. They are also the "moral authority," enforcing conformity. Finally, they are the spiritual authority in a world that recognizes no spiritual authority. Becoming a professional or a specialist is the only means of raising oneself above the ordinary.

There are three ways that the culture of professionals disables individuals and collapses the household. Professionals convert needs into deficiencies. In the preexisting culture of craftsmanship, need had a value. It was about relationship (before contract) that was organized by want, desire, obligation, and uniqueness within the community. Specialization inverts the idea of "need" itself. Need becomes an "absence" or "emptiness" located within the self. Chrematistic systems of exchange manufacture need-as-lack in order to increase the supply of services versus goods. Economics becomes the art of finding the deficiency in another person and servicing it for a fee.[7]

Secondly, specialization locates need within the needy—inside the boundary of the self. This is very important. Professionals perpetuate the illusion that people can be known as discrete wholes, without any attention paid to the contexts which form them. This form of stuck thinking is obvious, for example, in our conversation about mass migrations and the problems associated with them. Migrants are implicated in a much larger series of trends beyond their control: issues of legal status, availability of employment, the way that climate change impacts resource abundance, and the functionality of support systems in neighboring countries. The behaviors of a person who travels from one context to the other are determined by larger factors in the society that they leave and the society they arrive into. Yet specialized analysis focuses solely on migrants as individuals, as if there is not a ton of context that drives their choices. Individuals are part of a wider community of dependent relationships with the environment around them and the people who inhabit that environment. People are members of "socioeconomic-political" wholes. However, specialization looks at the individual outside of this context. Specialized professionals locate all problems within every individual as "an individual."[8]

Finally, specialization does not stop at the door of "the individual," but even individual humans are tended to by a variety of competing specialties that separate out the physical, the spiritual, and the mental. Within the physical this can be broken up into nose, eyes, throat, heart, blood, bone, etc. The young, middle aged, and old are grouped into specialized cohorts.[9] There are life coaches for work, doctors for the body, and spiritual specialists for the soul.

Illich sums up the effect of specialization within the chrematistic universe this way: "You are deficient, you are the problem, you have a collection of problems." The system makes money on "deficiency," where each human being is an "economic unit" with "multiple deficiencies" that must be treated for a fee.[10]

The Church has swallowed the lie that we exist to address people's spiritual deficiencies for a fee. We believe that our narrow purpose is to highlight people's sins and offer a tonic—participation in the Church. In the style of the chrematistic institutions we chase, we have converted individuals into pledging units. We have also siloed people into age groups with discrete deficiencies—children, youth, young adults, parents, and seniors. We have created programs that silo people based on gender—men's and women's Bible studies. We fancy ourselves arbiters of the spiritual for the individual and their many needs. And because society has bought into specialization and "need-as-deficiency," the Church that can convincingly provide such a cure does well.

William Stringfellow addresses this craze of specialization within the Church and points out that the clericalism that hampers our mission is part of our societal obsession with professionals and experts. The special skills that clergy learn in seminary become the basis of a false hierarchy of specialization. We have created a system where the baptized pursue their own disempowerment, and the clergy are complicit because their professional training encourages a paternalistic attitude toward the laity. This clericalism "aborts the edification of the people of the church and contradicts the servant character of the clergy's vocation."[11]

We would do well to remember that Dietrich Bonhoeffer believed that theology should be taught, learned, and practiced within a community furthering God's mission in the world. He rejects the ivory tower in favor of a missional community. Bonhoeffer believed that a community that follows Jesus could not be siloed away from the world. He points out that Jesus's community was characterized by "extraordinary visibility."[12]

Stringfellow laments that seminaries have become just like other schools churning out credentialed professionals. He believed that seminaries have lost the "confessional" aspect of being rooted inside a real, confessing, believing community. Seminaries separate students from such communities, removing them from the complex environment where they will serve, and where value is relational instead of need-based. I am not, along with Stringfellow, suggesting an end to seminary education, and I want to echo that there should be no "curtailment of the work of biblical scholarship."[13] In fact, we might multiply the theological training at seminary, and teach the history of Christian community in more detail. But all the teaching we do must be contextualized within the community where mission is lived out. Seminarians should not be sequestered. Learning communities that do not live within larger bodies doing the work of mission devolve into training camps for specialists and eventually undermine the reign of shalom that Christ is inaugurating. The seminary belongs to the mission of God as one of the principalities and powers that, if reclaimed, can be a powerful force for transformative mission.[14]

In Illich's essay from the 1970s, "Deschooling Society," he argues that "schooling" leads to "physical pollution, social polarization and psychological impotence."[15] He believes that schooling is a ritual where students receive special knowledge from professionals that enable their participation in a society based upon chrematistic systems of exchange. Such a culture of schooling makes individuals dependent upon educators, the system of specialization, and future professionals. We are trained out of the natural curiosity that helps us learn, and we lose our willingness to tolerate failure and the capacity to withstand criticism. We end up distrusting our natural capacities driven by curiosity and play. Illich believes that our institutional, disciplinary approach to learning has diminished our vision and hampered the kind of partnerships that foster hope in learning.[16] Learning is rooted in unrestricted curiosity within the context of meaningful relationships, where people are free to fail.

Illich's ideas are applicable to the Church and our approach to formation. We are constantly seeking the perfect universal program and the ideal packaged approach to Christian formation. We divide up age groups. We discipline curiosity. Older people who have been tempered in life and the young who are still naturally curious are separated from the middle aged who believe they have it all figured out. We have not offered people anything deeper than a youth group understanding of Jesus and yet we are baffled when the baptized lack any capacity for adaptation. We defend orthodoxy in a way that promotes uniformity instead of pointing people toward a more flexible, relational kind of unity. Our investment in disciplinary, institutional forms of learning have poorly prepared the Church for the emerging cultural shifts outlined above. We are ill equipped as the baptized and we are ill equipped as clergy.

In his book *The History of Theological Education,* Justo Gonzáles challenges the Church to see that theological education is not something that happens for three years after you have been selected for priesthood.[17] We must come to a shared understanding that there has never actually been one model of formation for the baptized. In fact, during the Church's period of greatest growth (that was not legally required by the Christian state), Christianity had no favored pedagogical model. There was a variety of views, texts, and ideas about God that coexisted in a messy way. Unity was prized more than uniformity. Moving forward, we will need to prepare

people to live within the community of peace by hewing closely to the ide-
als of the peaceable kingdom while rejecting learning models that make
good citizens of secular states. Christian formation will be about developing a lifelong character of "extraordinary visibility."[18]

Gonzáles also argues that seminaries should be more reflective institutions. Jesus tended to teach his disciples experientially, through doing and
then reflecting on what had been done. Gonzáles hopes that seminaries
can embrace an "action-reflection-action" model of formation.[19] Ambrose
and Augustine are exemplars of this form of formation, having been
schooled as philosophers and theologians who were forced to adapt their
theology and to their community contexts once they were in the practice
of ministry. Gonzáles's model benefits from being in keeping with the first
two to three centuries of practice. Historically the Church has done quite
well with a mix of book learning and practice. While Gonzáles focuses on
priestly training exclusively, I believe his model is useful for all kinds of
ministerial formation, particularly the formation of the baptized.

Gonzáles also reminds us that we need to address the issue of elitism in priestly training.[20] He is speaking about elitism in reference to the
clergy, but I want to weave in the baptized here. There is an elitist divide
between those who receive their master of divinity from a major university,
who get them from a seminary, and those trained through some kind of
alternative method. There is an elitist divide between the baptized over
who holds which professional position in the councils of the Church. This
elitism is a result of commodifying human life, viewing people as instru-
mental to the ends of institutional health and growth, and an ugly hunger
to compete with each other. We must name this elitism as an example of
the sibling rivalry that continues to infect the Church and acknowledge
that such uncharitable posturing is foreign to the Christian narrative and
inhibits our capacity to be the community of shalom. The question that
faces us now is how the clergy and the baptized can do ministry together,
hand in hand.

Finally, Gonzáles challenges our unspoken assumption that three-year
residential theological education is the only route to quality ministry. He
points out that study is a means of reaching a deeper understanding of God

and our relationship to him, not the fulfillment of a degree plan. He writes, "We study theology because we seek better to know and to serve the God whom we love—and this is a motivation equally present among the laity and not those ordained or seeking ordination."[21] Increasingly, people are finding different ways to be formed for ministry. The baptized want to be educated close to home so that they can be better ministers of the gospel. Shrinking resources combined with missional need is putting pressure on both the baptized and those in ordination tracks to get training in their local context. These trends will make the training programs of the future Church more diverse, rather than less.

In *Deschooling Society*, Illich recalls the story of Epimetheus, the brother of Prometheus. Together they represented the two extremes of humanity. Their job was to distribute their traits among the animals and humans. Epimetheus gave all the good traits to the animals and, because he did not think ahead, he had nothing left for humans. He is also the one who accepted the gift of Pandora's box. Prometheus saved the day with arts and fire. Illich writes, "Prometheus turned facts into problems, called necessity into question, and defied fate. Classical man framed a civilized context for human perspective. He was aware that he could defy fate-nature-environment, but only at his own risk."[22] Illich's point is that we have reversed what we gained from Prometheus and have returned to a way of life based upon Epimethean desire. When we see humans as deficient, we engage a way of life that puts production first and thought, reflection, and vision last.

We are the Epimethean human community, the Epimethean church community, born into a world of chrematistic exchange where all compete to satisfy the whims of appetite. Our formation and training is governed by fate, fact, necessity, and the needs of the Church principality. In our postmodern society, our schooling prepares everyone for his or her place as specialist and as deficient consumer. Even within the Church principality, we form people for a world of chrematistic exchange.[23] The Church has come to a crossroads because it barely resembles the vision God in Christ Jesus offered of a community of peace. Our chrematistic economy is increasingly oriented around the benefit of a few. Meanwhile, the Church has lost its luster. Theology is no longer the queen of the sciences, there are no more religious monarchies to legitimize, and we are becoming another manufacturer of need.

We are also left with a few questions about the Church's vocations. We know that in every age God has called and invited and the Church has listened and gone as God's representative. Sometimes the Church has ignored God's call and sometimes, despite itself, it has fulfilled God's invitation. Sometimes the Church has created something in its own image rather than God's. The future Church is no different, for even now we are searching for those who will answer the call tomorrow. So we ask, what are the shapes of those ministries? What are those new ways of going? Who are the leaders the future Episcopal Church needs? Who will give a clear and positive vision? Who will invite unity? Who will be the voice for the poor and innovate the service ministries? Who will create the new missionary tools for evangelism? Who has the courage to rethink stewardship? Who will help form the next generation of digital natives and self-learners? How do we think proactively about the whole body of the baptized? How do we rethink the way we form people through networks or relationships, online, and in person? How do we get theological education closer to the people? We are not looking for a new universal curriculum. We want these questions to guide us so that we can see more clearly the life-giving innovation that is already taking place in our church.

CHAPTER TWELVE

Ordered Future

We can walk as much as we want, we can build many things, but if we
do not profess Jesus Christ, things go wrong. We may become a charitable
NGO, but not the Church, the Bride of the Lord.

—Pope Francis[1]

A fellow bishop sent me a letter he found from one of his predecessors responding to a parishioner who had questioned his not wearing a mitre—that pointy hat worn by some bishops. The bishop explained that Episcopal vestments tell people about the kind of esteem we have for the different orders: bishops, priests, deacons, and laypeople. Episcopalians believe that bishops share in the councils of the Church along with our fellow ministers of the gospel—the baptized, the deacons, and the priests. We have a much more "democratically oriented type of Church polity."[2] He reminded his parishioner that prior to 1974 the mitre was rarely seen on a bishop because it was associated with the Byzantine emperor's crown—so much so that the Eastern bishops did not wear them until after the fall of Constantinople. The only time bishops were rumored to wear them in the Church of England was at the coronation of the king prior to the nineteenth century. He was kind and spoke of the genius of Anglicanism in allowing him to appreciate his remembrance of the tradition while his reader might have preferred another. I believe that the popularity of mitres among today's bishops is a sign of the growth of the power and hierarchy of the institutional Church. Mitres do not symbolize the collaborative ministry of Jesus or the democratic polity of our Church. Furthermore, the wearing of a mitre contravenes the theology of ordination innovated by the 1979 Book of Common Prayer.

In 1979, we changed the theology of ordination, Bishop Neil Alexander is fond of reminding new bishops.[3] Prior to 1979, the American Ordinal largely resembled the 1662 office, with a couple of changes that came by way of the Irish Book of Common Prayer. This previous ordinal indicated that bishops imparted some portion of their own "power" to the person being ordained. The 1979 Book of Common Prayer returns to the notion that the bishop is simply authorized by the community to do the particular work of ordination. A community gathers around its bishop and prays for a fresh outpouring of the Holy Spirit on the person to be ordained a priest. The bishop is the presider, the articulator, the animator, and the symbol of that action of the whole Church. Bishops say the words with the people, though the bishop may be the only one saying them aloud. I want you to understand this is a theological rejection of the popular idea that inside a bishop is a priest, inside a priest is a deacon, inside a deacon is a layperson or a subdeacon, as if they were Russian nesting dolls of ecclesial authority. Bishop Alexander reminds us that the 1979 prayer book is answering a twentieth-century question: "What is the church and how is it manifested in public assembly on the Lord's day?" He continues, "The 1979 prayer book was answering questions about things like, what does that assembly look like? Am I a passive member of that assembly who is fed, and has thanks distributed to me like sermons and communions and whatever else, or is my very presence there as a singer, as a prayer, as an intercessor . . . then they would begin to ask the questions again."[4] If we are to be aligned with the early Church, we must acknowledge that all participate together in consecrating holy things and people, but a few people have certain jobs that facilitate this work. It is not a complicated theology at all. When I wear the mitre, I worry that this theological principle is lost for those present. The fact of our total participation gives way, and the people play audience to an act between bishop and the ordinand.

We shall rest on the wise council of the previously mentioned bishop who concluded, "I believe we can respect each of these traditions and appreciate what each has to offer to the whole."[5] After all, this chapter is not about mitres. It is about the nature of the ordained ministry—our ordered future. Our theology of ordination should acknowledge that God invites the common people of God to engage in shalom making. They are to be a blessing and create communities of blessing. This work, carried out by the baptized, is supported by deacons, priests, and bishops.

We will begin with the work of bishops in the wider community. The faithful need bishops in order to do their work. Jesus had a purse keeper. The same was true for the protochurch as it emerged, and such purse keeping remained the primary work of the bishop in the first few centuries. I often say that the Church needs bishops to do the things laypeople do not want to do because they are not part of the primary mission. Bishops serve as a hub in the wheel of the Church, and help establish other hubs of mission through their bishoprics. Bishops should be unifying figures, at ease with their own beliefs and willing to listen to and make space for play theologically, liturgically, and prayerfully. Bishops hold the center so that flexing and growing can be normative for the local community.[6] Bishops hold fast to tradition, but acknowledge that all traditions are constructed.

In the future, bishops will continue to minister primarily through their presence in their communities and in the wider culture. They will maintain a see and cathedra,[7] but they will sit in the midst of their Christian communities and sit within the wider cultural context of their local communities. They will no longer be associated not only with their own church but also as a community member who desires the best for all the people who live in their diocese, and I do not mean only the Episcopalians. The people of any given area and of all denominations will know their local Episcopal bishop because that bishop is out and about. The presence of the bishop in the world outside of the church will be reminder of where the mission is to take shape. The bishop will be a celebrant of sacraments in the world and within the community. They will not lurk in ivory towers or diocesan centers. No matter what administrative duties befall them, the missional bishop remembers that they must go as an apostle to God's people where they are. The bishop models the essential missional practice of moving outside church walls, and meets the baptized missional leaders out there.

Bishops will also be responsible for raising up people from every walk of life, and of every profession, to take on the mission of the church. They will ordain priests and deacons, and discipline the Church's clergy. But missional bishops will use the ordination as a leverage point to ensure that there are many paths into ministry. They will send people to a diversity of programs and courses. Missional bishops will enable discernment for all people seeking out a vocation—not simply the clergy. Missional bishops will focus on the reign of peace, and the conversion of the world. They will measure their success by how well the baptized are living into their vocation. Missional bishops must be visionaries. They will work with each other to move the Church forward. The future bishop should be willing to raise a prophetic voice without shaking an impotent fist at the wider world. Words without deeds will be a foreign concept to the bishop of the future Church.

Missional bishops will believe, most of all, in the positive future of the Church, no matter the context. They will believe that God's kingdom of shalom is present in this world and has taken root like an oak of Mamre, growing even in the dust and clay of this world. They will have joined God on God's pilgrimage to reconcile the world and to bring about peace.

Missional bishops will also continue to study. They will be familiar with the scriptures and the life of Christ and the witness of the saints. They will seek revelation and vision from sources beyond the Church, because God in Christ is present in the world as well, drawing the world into communion. Bishops will study the world and understand the forces and people that animate it. They will speak the language of their mission context in order to proclaim a vision of the gospel of salvation to their people using symbols and images they understand.

Bishops of the Church will no longer be given authority or enjoy princely treatment because of their station. They will have to be servants of all, friends of many, and earn their authority with humility and a careful guiding hand. Bishops will increasingly be unable to operate by lording power over those in their care. They will have to work with them.

Bishops of the future will also need to be fluent in organizational complexity. Where diocesan organizations iterate a large set of structural features, the demands upon Episcopal leadership begin to change. Complexity allows small organizations to benefit by relationship with larger ones. Bishops who are fluent in complexity simplify difficulties and distribute overwhelming loads across many backs. They will use multidimensional matrices to spread resources efficiently and reduce costs for the whole. They will leverage the larger scale of a diocese to buy down the cost of doing business for parishes.[8] In order to achieve these gains, bishops in complex diocesan systems will need to do a variety of things all at once. They will learn to harness the energy of emergent actions through collaboration, ground level listening, making space for new mission to take shape, engaging people who live in our communities, and inviting open innovation.[9]

Let us turn our attention to the priest who models a local example of the fullness of Christ's work within the community of the baptized. Priests with reordered vocations understand their work as a symbol of God's work in and through Christ. Representing the bishop in a local context, the priest conveys the wider Church to the local community while providing crucial local context to the wider Church. I believe the role of the priest is undergoing a tremendous transformation. The priests of the future will be more connected to their people. Perhaps for the first time in over one hundred years, the pastoral and relational skills of the local priest and pastor will be their most essential gifts. Technological changes in how we communicate mean that priests will have a much larger capacity to be in touch with their parishioners. The amplification effect of social media means that priests of the future Church will have a whole crowd on their shoulder and in their phone with whom to communicate and share life. They will call that crowd their parish, congregation, or community. A priest's parish will not be defined by geographic boundaries, but will function as a more opened system with fluid boundaries. This change will redefine what it means to care for a congregation. No longer will "congregation" signify a building and the people who attend on any given Sunday. Missional priests will connect with people across the Christian community and across their mission context, making real world connections between church and what we have, in the past, designated "secular persons." For priests in the missional context, all people will be their people, the beloved of God.

The priest of the future Church will need to be a teacher, but standing in front of a congregation will no longer be the predominant way of teaching. The missional Church will call forward priests who connect people with resources and with other people, so that the self-learner can make their own learning pilgrimage. They will serve as guides and mentors in the process of self-learning by offering support to pilgrims that come in and out of their more porous, fluid communities. Missional priests will exhibit a posture of endless curiosity that is less about handing out answers and more about living with questions. Today we are emerging from a time when a single degree provided the necessary credentials for ministry. In the future the missional Church will license individuals based on their particular gifts and unique studies, rather than relying on a general, catch-all degree. I imagine that in many cases licensing will come after apprenticeship. Therefore the local priest will be responsible for forming the theo-curious among their cohort. But their means of formation will break free of the received "pupil/ student model" in favor of a more companionate pedagogy.

Missional priests will still be preachers. They will use the pulpit and small group settings, communicate throughout the web, text conversations, by uploading talks and videos, by sharing ideas throughout its network, and by every evolving means possible. Long gone are the days when proclaiming the gospel was the work of Sunday morning from a pulpit. The art of preaching will be the art of sharing stories and having conversations throughout the community. Like the first followers of Jesus who offered the story of Jesus to people in poor houses, in prison, on the roadside, and in the marketplace, the missional priest will be ever ready to proclaim the gospel by sharing the story of their own pilgrim journey and connecting with others.

The priest embracing their vocation will be ready to forgive. The priest of the future Church will talk about brokenness, sin, and falling away from God. They will be clear that there is always plenteous grace and redemption. They will offer forgiveness for the brokenness in the world. They will offer grace to all in their fluid, porous community. The future Church is ushering in a new focus on unconditional grace and forgiveness for all. In this new Christian community, there is wisdom about the complexities of life and the brokenness of human endeavors. Failings and flaws are understood as part of human life, and also the seat of creativity, initiative, and growth. The future priest will understand that when people fall and hurt themselves, others, and the environment, they need access to someone who will listen, understand, and declare God's forgiveness for them; so that they can gain greater self-awareness and amend their life accordingly.

The priest of the missional Church blesses people and the relationships that crisscross their fluid, porous community. The Church will have to be less controlling of the priest's ability to bless and be a part of people's lives. We will need to forsake our overly legal way of dealing with these issues. Such a law-based approach to the priest's pastoral ministry has empowered both ends of the spectrum who want to continue to fight over social issues, bullying one another with legislation and litmus tests. Priests will need to be trusted to do the good thing, the best thing for their people.

The priest of the future will also administer the rites of initiation for those who find their way into their community. Baptism will not be imprisoned in naves on Sunday mornings. The future priest will baptize anytime and anywhere baptism is desired. The priest will understand that baptism has had many forms throughout its history, and will use every opportunity and every form to baptize, as the self-directed pilgrim chooses. The priest of the future Church will understand that baptism is about the work of Christ that has already been doing, and it is for each person to decide when he or she is ready. We will practice open baptism as a missional church. The future priest will know that they are responsible for being prepared to baptize and so will baptize people in church on Sunday, in prison, at the hospital, and by the roadside and anywhere people discover that they are ready. The future Church will be invested in front door evangelism, in communication throughout its network, and in formation as a lifelong process, that it practices open baptism anytime anywhere for all people.

The priest will remain the chief sacramentalist for their community, celebrating and administering the Holy Eucharist. The priest will return to the ancient work of being the person who will celebrate on Sunday as they do today, and on sacred days and holidays. The future priest, though, will take the sacrament out of the Babylonian captivity where it resides today, at altars behind closed doors. The priest of the missional Church will take the bread and wine and go out into their mission context—out into the world—and celebrate the Eucharist. The local priest will work with other priests to ensure that all communities and congregations receive the sacrament as well, no matter how small or where it gathers: people's homes, nursing homes, community centers, in the back of an office, or in hospitals. They will understand that not everyone can come to the church, and so the sacrament will be taken out into the world. The Eucharist will be celebrated in just about every location imaginable. The present Church's idea that this happens in one place on Sunday morning will collapse in favor of expanding the Eucharistic reach of the fellowship of believers wherever they may be. I imagine it will have special significance as it returns to the common table where a meal is already being shared. I do not believe the missional Church will officially open the sacrament beyond a believer's meal for the baptized, but I also do not think the future Church will care much to actively police those boundaries. The leadership of a Church embracing its vocation will understand that God is so much bigger than canon and custom, but will not dispense with canon and custom all the same. God did a new thing through an old tradition of the *chabûrah* and now is doing a new thing through the expansion of table fellowship. New generations want to know what the boundaries are, so we should not hide them nor give up on our tradition; but we should not hang our mission upon them either. We know that God is at work wherever bread is broken and wine is shared. God is in the process of working and gathering his people.

The priest of the future Church will model the life of God in Christ Jesus by being out in the world. Jesus was an itinerant preacher, teacher, and sacramentalist. He made community wherever he went. Then he sent his followers out to do the same. He called them with their many vocations and taught them how to go out. He sent them to every kind of person, and he taught them to heal, forgive, and bless. Jesus inspired a sense of hope for a positive future for those who followed him AND for the whole world.

He wanted those who used his name and the name of God to have good news for every place and every people. The pattern of life that Jesus taught was pretty simple: love God, love your neighbor, do not hurt people, do not worry, and go. The priest of this gospel will not be stuck in their office, tied to their computer. Maintaining a mobile office from their car, coffee shop, or in other people's homes and workplaces, means that the priest of the future Church will be untethered from the church property; they will be an itinerant preacher, teacher, guide, and sacramentalist. The priests of the missional Church will work with many other priests and deacons to connect to people in their community. More formal relationships will create a thick web of productive, generative informal ones.

Some of these priests will have communities that grow out of current churches. Some will have several small communities in people's homes and workplaces. Still others will minister within work environments as missionaries to businesses, neighborhood community centers, hospitals, public schools, and communities designed for aging people. The priest of the future Church will be connected in the world and not tied to one geographical location—the church building. Some will manage large communities, with complex layers and disbursed smaller congregations connected to it. Priests of the future Church will inhabit many roles, in many places. Like Christ, they will simply go.

Finally, the role of deacons will be transformed in the future Church. Just as the vocation of the Church has turned inward during the last century, the role of the deacon has been focused inside the church building. Deacons have had increasingly less to do because of the nationalization of social services and the proliferation of NGOs. Deacons were once responsible for all who were in need. The deacon of the future Church will once more connect the Church's gospel message with the community and its needs. They will serve all people, but particularly the poor, the weak, the sick, and the lonely. And they will sacramentally model the work of the baptized through their service.

Deacons of the future Church will be skilled community organizers for the sake of the local church and the sake of the community. They will create new congregations and Christian communities, where the Church

is not already present. Deacons will preach and teach on behalf of the
Church, with a special focus on service to others. The deacons will start
new Christian communities in places where the poor have no advocates,
where the weak need help, and the sick and the lonely need aid and com-
panionship. Deacons will help the Church be healthy and well—so that
it resembles the reign of shalom. The deacon of the future Church will
connect members of the Christian community with members of the wider
community to discuss the community needs. They will use all the con-
nectivity and network power of the greater Church to bring resources to
bear for the benefit of the Church's neighbors for the resolution of conflict,
the creation of green space, to enhance the accessibility of services in the
neighborhood, provide access to clinics and preventative health care, and
clean up the community.

Deacons of the future Church will connect the needs of the people
(inside the community and outside the community) to the leaders of the
church (lay and ordained) so that those needs can be met. Because of the
connectedness of the deacons, the future Church will be known as a community that cares not only for one another but for its neighbors regardless
of denomination, faith, or belief system. Deacons will model the spirit of
Christ and the first disciples, who understood that the work is always to
love neighbor and to serve neighbor. Deacons will help the future Church
discard the old habit of throwing money at problems in favor of new models of mutual engagement.

I have attempted to demonstrate that the work of the three orders is to
model work that the baptized will do. This has always been the case. Clergy
will model and share and take people with them in their work. While there
are some specific tasks for clergy to do, the sausage-making that makes
lay ministry possible, the clergy's chief obligation is to join the baptized
and invite them to engage the vocation of the church as a community of
shalom at work in the world.

So who will serve in these roles? People of every age. There is a resur-
gence in ordinations of young people, but there will always be older people
ordained to the deaconate and priesthood as well, because longer life spans
and the trend toward second careers and multiple avocations means older

people are more often in the enviable position of reimagining the last third of their life from a position of strength. The bishops, priests, and deacons of the future Church will be full-time, part-time, and nonstipendiary, but the greater numbers will be part-time and nonstipendiary. There will be deacons and priests who are doctors, lawyers, mechanics, waiters, and hairdressers. There will also be full-time ordained vocations, and those clerics will undertake more complicated service in the wider church organization. More complex jobs will pay higher stipends in order to attract the best trained, educated, and future leaders. Nevertheless, pay scale diversity will grow over the next fifty years. In the future Church, the full-time ministers will be far outnumbered by the part-time ones. This will be true not because of a small and shrinking Church, but because the Church has relinquished control over vocations, because it will be growing while at the same time facing the high cost of maintaining buildings. The Church will eventually stop underwriting the employment of a vast number of clergy, instead using those dollars for local ministries and to achieve key missional objectives. We will not grow and then return to a full-time professionalized clergy and jettison these innovations. The Church will always have a core of full-time stipendiary clergy, but the new diversity of ordained vocations is here to stay and will most likely grow in influence. Without this diverse model of vocations, the mission of the Church is jeopardized. But even if we were to sell it all and walk away, we would end up hiring individuals to help manage the liquefied assets. Churches, structures outdated and new, buildings in various states of repair, and mission will mix with cost of energy, water, and cultural salary and benefit expectations to drive a mixed economy of full-time, part-time, and nonstipendiary ministers.

Our mission will birth Christian communities of various types, so clergy will work in a variety of contextual settings. In a suburban community, the future Church may be organized with a full-time priest serving with several nonstipendiary priests, who help with the wider sacramental and pastoral responsibilities of the growing community and its multiple sites. Meanwhile in the same parish community, a nonstipendiary priest and several deacons might be out starting new communities in underserved areas, and creating service connections throughout the surrounding neighborhood. In an urban context, we might find a nonstipendiary priest and deacon working in a slum, or poorer part of town, to build up a Christian community around an organized project like a community garden to provide fresh fruit and vegetables in the middle of a food desert.

.   They might be sponsored and connected with a larger community like the one mentioned above or they might be stand-alone. A large urban parish may have several full-time priests and deacons, an army of nonstipendiary clergy, a host of lay preachers, pastors, and administrators, who oversee multiple mission sites, and a variety of small congregation/communities across the whole city. Still, a small community congregation may have a full-time priest or be served by an urban or suburban nonstipendiary leader. All of these ministry sites of the future Church will build ministry capacity by sharing administration and overhead. There will be bishops who oversee several dioceses. Nonstipendiary and part-time bishops will join them to increase pastoral reach. Gone is the concern about the number of bishops representing dioceses. Missionary bishops working in teams and sharing episcopal authority will replace the "full-time one bishop to a diocese" model. Bishops will raise up and call forth a diverse clergy and lay population focused on the mission of the new Church. There will be bishops who hold positions as heads of congregations and large urban communities. There will be bishops who travel to support new ministry contexts where various creative and innovative styles of leadership are needed to propel ministry forward. There is no one solution that will define how the future Church carries out its ministry. It will do all things necessary for the sake of the God's mission of shalom.

CHAPTER THIRTEEN

The Gap

We worshipped Jesus instead of following him on his same path. We made Jesus into a mere religion instead of a journey toward union with God and everything else. This shift made us into a religion of "belonging and believing" instead of a religion of transformation.

—Richard Rohr[1]

After the revelation of the Ten Commandments in Exodus, God invited Moses back up the mountain.[2] Moses was delayed in coming back down. He was gone for a very long time. In fact, some translations imply it was an excruciatingly long time. So the people did what people do all the time—in the absence of leadership and God, they made an idol. God got upset at their idolatry. Moses got angry and smashed the tablets with the Ten Commandments. Aaron offered a lame excuse and blamed the people, scapegoating them for his failure of judgment. I have always assumed that this story is about totems for idol worship, maybe because I was so affected by the Cecil B. DeMille movie *The Ten Commandments*. I assumed that the Israelites chose another god—the golden calf. After all, Aaron does say, "Here is your god!"

The eleventh-century Rabbi Abraham Ben Meir Ibn Ezra anticipated my confusion. He taught that the idol was not made to take God's place, but Moses's. The idol was to be the means by which the people could commune with God, in the absence of a leader. I discovered this interpretation in an article by Rabbi Josh Gerstein, who also quoted Rabbi J. B. Soloveitchik, one of the great twentieth-century Jewish thinkers, who wrote:

> They felt that they themselves did not have access to the Almighty. Only somebody of great charisma and ability could have access to him. The people sinned because they were perplexed. Moses has been gone for a long time. . . . They did not understand that, while Moses was the greatest of all prophets and the greatest of all men, every Jew has access to God. . . . Sometimes it is a sense of one's greatness that causes sin; sometimes it is a sense of one's smallness.[3]

Finally, Rabbi Jonathan Sacks, the former chief rabbi of England, put it eloquently, "Every Jew is an equal citizen of the republic of faith because every Jew has access to its constitutional document, the Torah."[4] The people did not understand that God was personally in relationship to them. God brought them out of Egypt in order that they might be free and continue to be a blessed people and a blessing to the world around them. God did not need any go-betweens, not Moses and not golden calves.

The story of the golden calf is about the human tendency to believe that human-made items can resolve our fear, anxiety, sense of lostness, despair, and hopelessness. The calf was supposed to be a conduit of grace. But God's work of shalom is about relationship. God invites God's people directly to go on God's behalf, so God can do mighty works through them. No golden calf is necessary. No object is needed for the relationship between God and God's people to take root in the world—only a community of willing individuals.

I think we Christians have made our churches into golden calves out of our well-meaning desire for relationship with the divine. Doing church has become the idol we hope God will use to save us. But the God we worship invites us into something quite different. We are willing to say, "Yes, I will go" to church. But will we go on God's behalf into the world to relate with others? Will we be Christ's body in the world for God? God asks, "Who will go for us?" If we answer "yes," we are signing up for much more than church attendance. We are signing up to make communities that are not marred by endless jostling for authority and power. These communities will be places where people can enjoy direct relationship to God in their relationships with each other. False dichotomies like "we and them" or "inside and outside" slip away. We think that the Church is a means to God rather than one space where relationship with God can happen. But God's invitation into relationship through Christ and the Cross can be lived out in any community. In other words the way to God is through our brothers and sisters.

> In Christianity, the non-dual paradox and mystery was a living person, an icon we could gaze upon and fall in love with. Jesus became the "pioneer and perfecter of our faith" (Hebrews 12:2), "the Mediator," "very God and very human" at the same time, who consistently said, 'follow me.' He is the living paradox, calling us to imitate him, as we realize that "[he] and the Father are one" (John 10:30). In him, the great gaps are overcome; all cosmic opposites are reconciled in him, as the author of Colossians says so beautifully (1:15–20).[5]

God has been telling us since the time of Abraham and Sarah that nothing is necessary but relationships and the road. God has made "one out of two"—without religion to get in the way. We repeatedly choose religion and worship instead of following our Lord into the world where we will find God with others.

Our work, our calling, is citizenship in a reign of shalom that has been prepared for us since the very foundations of the cosmos were set in place. Living outside of the false paradox offered by the powers will mean living into our completeness and our otherness. We will be more like the ecclesia of the apostles, the first motley crew of Jesus followers. We will be the community of peace imagined on the road to Emmaus.

God's call reaches all humanity—a dragnet that catches all the refuse of creation. God has called the ordinary people of God the *hoi palloi* and made them the *sanctum populus dei*. God sends us in God's name to go and bless God's friends. We share this vocation of peace with each other. This vocation has sprung from Christ's Cross on Golgotha, and its branches reach the margins of society where the greatest misfits are found. We are invited to see our ordinary existence within the created community of

God, and are called to accept our particular role in bringing about God's future. There is a seamlessness to this salvific narrative that weaves together all things that were once divided.

The Great Commission is not a New Testament "add on," but a foregrounding of a theme embedded in God's dealings with humanity from the very beginning. God is not in the religion business. Equations of religious salvation are man-made idols that end with scapegoating and violence. If God were that kind of lesser God, Abraham's sacrifice of Isaac would have been accepted. In the end the only sacrifice God accepts is the sacrifice of ourselves. Paul emphasizes this fact as he exhorts the Romans to "present your bodies as a living sacrifice" (Rom. 12:1). Religious institutions imagine vocation as a sacrificing of some other, something outside of the self. Our vocation from God and conveyed through scripture is a sacrifice of self, comfort, and safety.

In choosing ordinary people to be God's people, God breaks human myths about power and authority. Through the handiwork of ordinary people invited into extraordinary work, God inverts the mythic story of a new society made with violence. The vocation of the Church can never be violence, but only an act of service and love. Accepting God's call means correcting the violent ontological distortion that haunts modern secular society. As long as we continue to define the world through "me," which is buffered and separate from "you," then we submit to the ritual, religious bloodletting of ancient sibling rivalry. The history of violence can only be undone if we contextualize our vocations in the midst of Christ's one body first, and focus on our unique parts second. Partnering with God, we cease to see a partitioned world of buffered people. By rejecting this "I get mine, you get yours" religion, we stop mistaking our faith as a means of compelling others to become something they are not: me. At the very core, saying "yes" to God is about becoming a whole of paradoxically interdependent parts.

God's invitation to vocation also erodes the compartmentalization between our religious and professional lives. In the biblical worldview, the way of peace requires full participation. We cannot claim to be one person in one particular context or set of relations, and then claim to be a totally different person in another context. There is no such thing as professional holy people. We live complete lives in continuity with God and our vocation is equally operative in every space we inhabit.

I long to animate the paralyzed vocations within the Church by destroying the notion that vocations only exist at the altar where we turn our backs to the world. Our desire for institutional permanence does great damage to Christ's mission. When institutional survival is our chief concern, violence warps the vessel that is meant to carry the gospel. And yet, there is no way to shed institution in all its forms. But we can bind the institution to the mission it is intended to serve. We can make the institutional church into an exemplary principality. We have received this Church as a gift, so we need to use it as a transformative tool for the work of mission.

We will need to share meals with people of all kinds so that true relationships flower in our communities. The norm is to eat with our like-minded cohorts. Our kingdom-like meals must be transgressive, meaning that the table is shared openly with a diversity of people with whom we would not normally dine. We tend to avoid the scandal of dining with folks of every kind and, if we are honest, the most religious parts of our hearts believe there is something not quite right about that practice to begin with. Yet the early church did exactly as Jesus did. The apostles overrode their own religious instincts and ate with detested people. When people were starving and in need, they did not waste energy trying to convince the powers and authorities to feed them. They gave them something to eat.

I love the Church, and the Episcopal Church most of all. It has saved my life and guided me through very difficult times. It helps me understand God's love for me, and God's invitation into a new relationship. The Church has been a gift to me and I want to share the best of it with others. But it must be reformed, revived, and transformed. In order to live in the new mission age that is before us, the Church will have to recover an old understanding of vocation rooted out in the world where God makes peaceable community. The Church will have to discard its inward focus and become a guiding light in the world outside the walls of our precious buildings.

I want to share one last image of God's invitation. Let us think about the Church as a boat. Early Christian writing, as in the homily attributed to Peter found in the letters of Clement, used this image: "For the whole business of the Church is like unto a great ship, bearing through a violent storm men who are of many places, and who desire to inhabit the city of the good kingdom."[6] Church-as-boat grew in popularity so that by the fourth century, the nautical term "nave" was associated with church architecture. Nave means boat. A church looks like an upside-down boat. When we play with this image, we think about church-as-boat being a refuge and sanctuary. But when we turn to scripture, and especially the New Testament, the boat is a place from which people are called. Jesus called the fishermen from the boat to follow him. And at the end of the Gospels, Jesus again called them from the boat to join him on the seashore and go into all the lands. Jesus called Peter from the boat to walk on water, even though Peter did not want to get out. Peter got out and sank. Jesus was there and lifted him up. That story is about Jesus's invitation to get out of the boat no matter what it costs. The invitation to us today is to get out of the boat and leave our church buildings.

Boats also get people places. Jesus taught from boats, and used them to go from one place to another. But boats were never used as shelter. They were not permanent places of God's presence. They were a means of conveyance. The body of Christ, the Church in this world, is a means by which God in Christ Jesus gets from one place to another. That Church is made up of the living people who make up Christ's body. We are the Church and we go with Christ into the world. The Church is not a temple where God dwells and humans come to meet him.

Finally, the New Testament makes clear that if we stay in the boat, there will be stormy seas and we will argue. Staying in the boat too long will even put Jesus to sleep! Living with an inward focus and making our vocations a means of perpetuating our own institutional structures is a sure way to end up in a family feud. The only cure for such sibling rivalry is Jesus and his mission.

We are only just waking up to discover the ages of Constantine and the Reformation are over. In this five hundredth year anniversary of the

Reformation, we have discovered that our efforts are uncreative, repetitive, and divided. We repeat the patterns and hope for different results. There is a gap between where we are and what we say we believe, but the potential for realignment with God's invitation is continuous. God hopes we will bridge the gap between the Church and the reign of peace. God hopes to breach the church walls that separate us from creation. God calls us to put aside our fear and anxiety, gird ourselves with gospel courage and step across the illusionary chasm that lulls us into inaction. William Willimon, a retired Methodist minister, tells the following story:

> So that's the way I think about the gap. After one of my lectures, one of my classes, when I got finished I came out and this young, earnest, sweet young man came up to me and said, "Hey, did you ever think about leaving the Methodist church because you seem unhappy?" I said, "Oh, gosh. Maybe I overdid the critique on this." I said to the young man, "No, I didn't think about it. I didn't think about losing it any more than when I found out my mother was not the greatest person in the world to have as a mother. You're kind of stuck here. Even in my critique of the Methodist church, I think I'm being very Methodist. And I'm showing this church has had its way with me, and I keep wanting more."

There has always been and will always be a gap between God's call and our response. I, like Willimon and a host of others, can see it and want to talk about it as part of a journey into God's creation for the sake of God's mission. We must face the gap between God's call and our institutional reality. I try to do this in a very Episcopal way. God beckons us to make a very different kind of worldly community. We are invited into God's reign of shalom in this world, a reign that brings the bloody, ancient practice of sibling rivalry to an end. This is the Church's true vocation.

Acknowledgments

I am grateful to the Episcopal Diocese of Texas and its people who continue to press me into conversations about the future mission of the church and why it matters. I am grateful for the support of my staff that enables me to have time to write. The Rev. John Newton especially has been supportive of the work and an encourager along the way, as has the Rev. Canon Kai Ryan. My first reader and conversation partner for this book was the Rev. Patrick Hall, who has my gratitude for the work and time he put into the book, and the gratitude of my wife, JoAnne, who served as the first reader for the last five books.

Of course there is Milton Brasher-Cunningham, my editor, and the team at Church Publishing who are always wonderful to work with and supportive of my projects. Without them I would not be able to bring the text to life.

Finally, I am grateful to JoAnne, who knows I sneak off to the desk in the early morning hours and late at night to work on my writing and who is always caring, encouraging, and excited to hear what is next.

Notes

Foreword

1. Stanley Hauerwas, *A Community of Character: Toward a Constructive Christian Social Ethic* (Notre Dame: University of Notre Dame, 2010), 3.

Introduction

1. Eschatology is the theology of the end of all things. Eschaton is literally the culmination of God's plan. William Stringfellow, *Dissenter in a Great Society: A Christian View of America in Crisis* (Nashville, TN: Abingdon, 1966), 142.
2. William Stringfellow, *A Keeper of the Word: Selected Writings of William Stringfellow,* ed. Bill Wylie Kellermann (Grand Rapids, MI: W. B. Eerdmans, 1994), 31, 305.
3. Neil Alexander, "The Bishop and the Liturgy," class discussion, Living Our Vows: Episcopal Church Bishop Residency, Roslyn Conference Center, Richmond, Virginia, June 15, 2017. See also, Alexander, "Practical Ecclesiology: Reflections on Anglican Eucharistic Faith and Practice," in *Drenched in Grace: Essays in Baptismal Ecclesiology,* ed. Lizette Larson-Miller and Walter Knowles (Eugene, OR: Pickwick Publications, 2013), 197.
4. In *The Jesus Heist,* I make a distinction between a temple-oriented faith associated with Mount Zion and the Sinai wilderness tradition. I firmly believe that Jesus was rooted in the Sinai tradition and that we must recover this tradition if we are to take mission seriously in the twenty-first century.

Chapter One

1. Walter Brueggemann, "Evangelism and Discipleship: The God Who Calls, the God Who Sends," *Word and World* 24, no. 2 (2004): 121–35.

2. A full treatment of this idea of "wilderness" transformation can be found in *The Jesus Heist*.

3. Brueggemann, "Evangelism," 122.

4. Ibid., 123.

5. The Roman Catholic document the *Lineamenta*, n15, defines vocation in this way: "Vocation is broader than mission because it is composed of both a call to *communio* and a call to mission. *Communio* is the fundamental aspect destined to endure forever. Mission, on the other hand, is a consequence of this call and is limited to an earthly existence." Kenyan B. Osborne, *Ministry: Lay Ministry in the Roman Catholic Church, Its History and Theology* (Eugene, OR: Wipf & Stock, 2003), 597.

6. Brueggemann, "Evangelism," 125.

7. Jonathan Sacks, "Bereishit (5769)—Violence in the Name of G-d," Office of Rabbi Sacks, October 25, 2008, http://rabbisacks.org/covenant -conversation-5769-bereishit-violence-in-the-name-of-g-d/.

8. Brueggemann, "Evangelism," 125. This is how Gideon experiences God, as pure peace, shalom. Gideon was one of Israel's judges and built an altar and called it, "The LORD is peace" (Judg. 6:24). God's work is this shalom, and God calls upon God's people to enact it by going.

9. Jonathan Sacks, "Freewill (Vaera 5775)." Rabbi Sacks Office, January 12, 2015, http://rabbisacks.org/freewill-vaera-5775/.

10. Sacks, "Freewill".

11. Brueggemann, "Evangelism," 125.

12. Ibid., 126.

13. Stanley Hauerwas and Travis Reed, "What Is A Christian?" The Work of the People, 2012, accessed July 20, 2017, http://www.theworkofthepeople.com /what-is-a-christian.

14. I am adapting here Hauerwas's theology of community as the underlying work of God in the shalom community. Just as Hauerwas repeatedly reminds us that the raising of you and me is linked to Jesus and then Israel's freedom, so too then is our community of shalom today rooted deeply in the call of the people of Israel paradigmatically seen in the lives of Abraham and Sarah, Esther, Isaiah, and Jonah. For that matter, it is the story of the book itself as we will see when we come to the story of Jesus. Hauerwas, *Community*.

15. Hauerwas, *Community*, 3.

16. Ibid., 2.

17. Ibid., 3.

18. Brueggemann, "Evangelism," 126.

19. See Jonathan Sacks's book *Not in God's Name: Confronting Religious Violence*. Jonathan Sacks, *Not in God's Name: Confronting Religious Violence* (New York:

Schocken, 2017). See Emily McNeill's "Rabbi Jonathan Sacks Explores Roots of Religious Violence," *Cornell Chronicle*, April 21, 2016, http://news.cornell .edu/stories/2016/04/rabbi-jonathan-sacks-explores-roots-religious-violence. See also Brian McDonald, "Violence & the Lamb Slain," *Touchstone Archives: Violence & the Lamb Slain*, December 2003, http://www.touchstonemag.com /archives/article.php?id=16-10-040-i.

Here follows Girard's version of this idea, which Sacks is dependent upon when he is speaking about the subject of "sibling rivalry" as the root of human violence. "We must establish first of all that there are two kinds of sacrifice. Both forms are shown together in the story of Solomon's judgment in the third chapter of 1 Kings. Two prostitutes bring a baby. They are doubles engaging in a rivalry over what is apparently a surviving child. When Solomon offers to split the child, the one woman says 'yes,' because she wishes to triumph over her rival. The other woman then says, 'No, she may have the child,' because she seeks only its life. On the basis of this love, the king declares that 'she is the mother.' Note that it does not matter who is the biological mother. The one who was willing to sacrifice herself for the child's life is in fact the mother. The first woman is willing to sacrifice a child to the needs of rivalry. Sacrifice is the solution to mimetic rivalry and the foundation of it. The second woman is willing to sacrifice everything she wants for the sake of the child's life. This is sacrifice in the sense of the gospel. It is in this sense that Christ is a sacrifice since he gave himself 'for the life of the world.' What I have called 'bad sacrifice' is the kind of sacrificial religion that prevailed before Christ. It originates because mimetic rivalry threatens the very survival of a community. But through a spontaneous process that also involves mimesis, the community unites against a victim in an act of spontaneous killing. This act unites rivals and restores peace and leaves a powerful impression that results in the establishment of sacrificial religion. But in this kind of religion, the community is regarded as innocent and the victim is guilty. Even after the victim has been "deified," he is still a criminal in the eyes of the community (note the criminal nature of the gods in pagan mythology)."

20. Hauerwas, *Community*, 2.
21. Brueggemann, "Evangelism," 121.

Chapter Two

1. Richard Rohr and Travis Reed, "Bearing the Divine Through the Ordinary," The Work of the People, 2014, accessed July 22, 2017, http://www.theworkof thepeople.com/bearing-the-divine-through-the-ordinary.
2. I typically use NRSV in the texts from scripture. Here I am translating and using my own word study.

3. René Girard, *Things Hidden Since the Foundation of the World* (Stanford, CA: Stanford University Press, 1987), 215–23.

4. Girard, *Hidden*, 221.

5. The complete absence of any sexual element has nothing to do with repression—an explanation thought up at the end of the nineteenth century and worthy of the degraded puritanism that produced it. The fact that sexuality is not part of the picture corresponds to the absence of the violent mimesis with which myth acquaints us in the form of rape by the gods. This idol—what we have called the model-obstacle—is completely absent. Girard, *Hidden*, 222.

6. Jason Porterfield, "The Subversive Magnificat: What Mary Expected the Messiah to Be Like," Enemy Love, January 19, 2013, http://enemylove.com/subversive-magnificat-mary-expected-messiah-to-be-like/.

7. Dietrich Bonhoeffer, *The Mystery of the Holy Night*, ed. Manfred Webber (New York: Crossroad, 1996), 6. The text was translated originally by Peter Heinegg from Bonhoeffer, *Werke*, vol. 9.

8. Charles Taylor, *A Secular Age* (Cambridge, MA: Belknap Press of Harvard University Press, 2007), 775.

9. Ibid., 774.

10. Ibid., 542.

11. Ibid., 543.

12. Robert Bellah, "Religious Evolution," *American Sociological Review* 29 (1964): 358–74, http://www.jstor.org/stable/2091480?origin=JSTOR-pdf&seq=1#page_scan_tab_contents.

13. The Rev. Sam Wells is the first person I know of who used the term "Nazareth Manifesto" in his essay by the same name. Wells offers that Jesus did not simply offer a word of release for the captives and food for the poor, Jesus seeks to be with the people in their hunger and imprisonment. Sam Wells, "Nazareth Manifesto," *Vagt Lecture: The Nazareth Manifesto*, April 27, 2008, https://web.duke.edu/kenanethics/NazarethManifesto_SamWells.pdf.

14. Charles L. Campbell, *The Word before the Powers: An Ethic of Preaching* (Louisville, KY: Westminster John Knox, 2002), 49.

15. Walter Wink, *Engaging the Powers: Discernment and Resistance in a World of Domination* (Minneapolis, MN: Fortress Press, 1999), 112.

16. See also John Kavanaugh's discussion of the link between violence and the commodity form of life in *Following Christ in a Consumer Society*, John F. Kavanaugh, *Following Christ in a Consumer Society: The Spirituality of Cultural Resistance* (Maryknoll, NY: Orbis Books, 2006) 43–53.

17. Stanley Hauerwas, *The Peaceable Kingdom: A Primer for Christian Ethics* (Notre Dame: University of Notre Dame Press, 2011), 118.

18. Brian McDonald, An Interview with Rene Girard, "Violence & the Lamb Slain," Touchstone Archives: Violence & the Lamb Slain, December 2003, accessed July 24, 2017, http://www.touchstonemag.com/archives/article.php ?id=16-10-040-i.]

19. Walter Wink, *Engaging the Powers Discernment and Resistance in a World of Domination* (Minneapolis, MN: Fortress Press, 1999), 102.

20. Wink, *Engaging*, 102.

Chaper Three

1. William Alexander Percy, *Enzio's Kingdom, and Other Poems* (New Haven, CT: Yale University Press, 1924), 9. The poem "His Peace" appeared in 1924, and the last four verses became the hymn "They Cast Their Nets in Galilee" present in *The Hymnal 1982* with the Georgetown tune, composed by David McWilliams.

2. I first understood this concept when I read scholar and activist Ched Myers's commentary on Mark entitled *Binding the Strong Man*. In it Myers claims the term "fishers of men" is not about "saving souls" but about "overturn(ing) the existing order of powers, and privilege." The problem I have with Myers's reading is that at times it devolves into a humanistic justice argument willing to accept violence. I also think that it is too focused on social action and does not take into account the overarching theme of the cross, resurrection, and salvation as a cosmic undoing and redoing. I am offering here a different version—one with a critical eye to Myers's reading, though clearly indebted to it. Ched Myers, *Binding the Strong Man: A Political Reading of Mark's Story of Jesus* (Maryknoll, NY: Orbis Books, 2008), 132.

3. Walter W. Skeat, *An Etymological Dictionary of the English Language* (Oxford: Clarendon Press, 1897), 689. It also had to do with the company one kept, or the community in which one was a part. It was about the people with whom you gathered. Skeat, *Etymological*, 575.

4. See also Gustaf Wingren, *Luther on Vocation*, trans. Carl C. Rasmussen (Eugene, OR: Wipf & Stock Publishers, 2004). Also, David L. Jeffrey, *A Dictionary of Biblical Tradition in English Literature* (Grand Rapids, MI: Wm. B. Eerdmans, 1992). See also Max Weber, *The Protestant Ethic and the Spirit of Capitalism*, trans. Talcott Parsons (Kettering, OH: Angelico Press, 2014). 79.

5. See Mark Starr and George Barker, *A Worker Looks at History: Being Outlines of Industrial History Specially Written for Labour College-Plebs Classes* (London: Plebs League, 1919).

6. Robert Farrar Capon, *Kingdom, Grace, Judgment: Paradox, Outrage, and Vindication in the Parables of Jesus* (Grand Rapids, MI: W.B. Eerdmans, 2002), 113–15.

7. Ibid.. 113.
8. Ibid., 115.
9. There are multiple theologies of atonement that are accepted within ortho-
dox Christianity. Most people are familiar with the one where God requires
Jesus to be a blood sacrificed. If you are interested in the many theologies of
the Christian Church. I suggest reading *The Crucifixion: Understanding the
Death of Jesus Christ* by Fleming Rutledge (Grand Rapids, MI: William B.
Eerdmans, 2017). This is an excellent text on the subject.
10. Capon, *Kingdom*, 115.
11. Ibid.
12. Ibid.
13. Ched Myers, "Mark: Invitation to Discipleship," in *The New Testament:
Introducing the Way of Discipleship*, ed. Sharon Ringe and Wes Howard-Brook
(Maryknoll, NY: Orbis Books, 2002), 9.
14. Ched Myers, "Jesus' 'Second Call' to Discipleship," Radical Discipleship,
Feburary 26, 2015, https://radicaldiscipleship.net/2015/02/26/jesus-second
-call-to-discipleship/.
15. Ibid.
16. Ibid.

Chapter Four

1. Dietrich Bonhoeffer, *Life Together*, trans. John W. Doberstein (San Francisco:
Harper SanFrancisco, 1954), 100.
2. In his essays on Christian community, Stringfellow writes well on its nature,
which I believe closely follows not only Stringfellow and Bonhoeffer's
ideas of a confessional community, but closely reveal the arc of the narrative through the book of Acts. Therefore, I am using Stringfellow's
thoughts to outline what I see in the book of Acts. William Stringfellow
in James Walters, "William Stringfellow (LSE 1949-50)—a Christian,
Not a Moralist," LSE History: London School of Economics and Political
Science, June 2016, http://blogs.lse.ac.uk/lsehistory/2016/02/04/william
-stringfellow-lse-1949-50-a-christian-not-a-moralist/.
3. Stringfellow wrote, "To be a Christian has, rather, to do with that peculiar
state of being bestowed upon men [sic] by God. . . . It has to do with that form
of self-acceptance which is a gift of God and not something achieved or sustained." James Walters, chaplain to the London School of Economy writing
on Stringfellow's leadership, reflects, "This is one expression of Stringfellow's
resolute conviction that to associate Christianity closely with any moral stance
is to reduce the Gospel to some ideology." Walters, *Stringfellow*.

4. William Stringfellow, "The Politics of Pastoral Care: An Ecumenical Meditation concerning the Incumbent Pope," in *Keeper of the Word*, ed. Bill Wylie Kellerman (Grand Rapids, MI: William B. Eerdmans, 1994), 286.

5. Stringfellow ("Acolytes of the Demonic Powers," in *Keeper*, 274) characterizes how the institution works in this way:

> In truth, the conspicuous moral fact about our generals, our industrialists, our scientists, our commercial and political leaders is that they are the most obvious and pathetic prisoners in American society. There is unleashed among the principalities in this society a ruthless, self-proliferating, all-consuming institutional process that assaults, dispirits, defeats, and destroys human life even among, and *primarily* among, those persons in positions of institutional leadership. They are left with titles but without effectual authority; with the trappings of power but without control over the institutions they head; in nominal command but bereft of dominion. These same principalities, as has been mentioned, threaten and defy and enslave human beings of other status in diverse ways, but the most poignant victim of the demonic in America today is the so-called leader.

6. Ibid.

7. The story of Lydia is one of my new favorites. There is a great text that illustrates her place in the overarching narrative. For further study, read Alexandra Gruca-Macaulay, *Lydia as a Rhetorical Construct in Acts* (Atlanta: SBL Press, 2016).

8. There is debate about the primacy of baptism and the laying on of hands by apostolic representatives. These two sacraments are the primary acts of entry into Christian community.

9. I want to be careful to not overstate the case for a lack of sacred texts. It's clear from the Christ hymn in Philippians, which is considered by some to be a fragment of a baptismal liturgy that Paul assumed the community at Philippi would be familiar with, that there were hymns, and perhaps even liturgies shared between early Christian communities. But to believe that there were many hymns and whole liturgies as we think of them today is hindsight bias. Yes, in 1 Corinthians, Paul alludes to the Eucharistic instruction that he handed down to the Corinthian church, including the words of institution. The fact that Colossians, Ephesians, and the Pastoral Epistles were written in Paul's name indicates that his letters were copied and widely shared among the early churches. Hebrews also gives evidence of the sort of circular sermons that were swapped between the early churches. Also, Luke and Matthew

clearly had copies of Mark to consult when they wrote their Gospels, and there is no reason to suspect there weren't still other copies wandering around the early church. However, hindsight bias looks back and amplifies these facts, often leading to an assumption that the early church was a liturgical church in the same sense that today's church is a liturgical church, or that the early church had access to scripture in the same manner that today's church can access scripture. We forget that the masses in the first century were uneducated, could not read or write, and that formal training was not present for the clergy. Therefore, I err on the side of many communities and few manuscripts. By the time we get to the second century and we have an urban movement, we certainly see more manuscripts and common liturgies, but not in the early to mid-first century when Paul traveled as a missionary and the budding ecclesia began to flower.

10. N. T. Wright does a wonderful job as he explains this fine point (N. T. Wright, "Jesus' Resurrection and Christian Origins," NTWrightPage, accessed July 31, 2017, http://ntwrightpage.com/2016/07/12/jesus-resurrection-and-christian-origins/. Originally published in *Gregorianum* 83, no. 4 (2002): 615–35). He writes:

> This almost complete absence of a spectrum of belief itself demands explanation, but before we can offer one we must add two further points. First, the early Christian belief in resurrection had a much more precise shape and content than anything we find in Judaism. In early Christianity, obviously in Paul but not only there, resurrection will be an act of new creation, accomplished by the Holy Spirit, and the body which is to be is already planned by God. This will not be a simple return to the same sort of body as before; nor will it be an abandonment of embodiedness in order to enjoy a disembodied bliss. It will involve transformation, the gift of a new body with different properties. This is so engrained in earliest Christianity that it already affects teaching on other subjects, such as baptism (Romans 6) and ethics (Colossians 3).
>
> Where did that idea come from? Not from any ancient paganism known to us; and not, or not straightforwardly, from any ancient Judaism. The best-known feature of resurrection in Daniel 12 is that the righteous will shine like stars; that, interestingly, is one thing the early Christians do *not* say about the hope of resurrection, except in one gospel passage (Matthew 13.43) not echoed elsewhere. The hope of resurrection is thus not only virtually universal in early Christianity; it is much more sharply focused than its Jewish equivalent.

You may wish to read further, in which case I suggest Wright's, "Resurrection in Q?" in *Christology, Controversy & Community: New Testament Essays in Honour of David R. Catchpole*, ed. D. G. Horrell and C. M. Tuckett (Leiden: Brill, 2001), 85–97. I also think that the essay entitled *Against S. J. Patterson, The God of Jesus: The Historical Jesus and the Search for Meaning* (Harrisburg, PA: Trinity Press International, 1998), ch. 7 specifically is worth a look. The primacy of the resurrection in the early teachings of those who followed is essential.

11. Matthew 26:17–30; Mark 14:22–24; Luke 13:26; Luke 22:19–20; John 6:35; John 6:51; John 6:53–57; John 13:1–4; Acts 2:42; Acts 2:46–47; Acts 20:7; 1 Corinthians 10:16–17; 1 Corinthians 10:21–22; 1 Corinthians 11:20–34.

12. Scholars debate the use of the words of institution and their purpose in the early Christian communities. By the time we get to the second century and the text of Christian instruction entitled *The Didache* and the early church theologian Justin Martyr, there is a suggestion that the words of institution were not used in the celebration of the Supper even at that time. Justin Martyr writes of them but is clear that they are used for instruction of the baptized instead of during a rite. Martyr writes that these words are important so as to understand the breaking of bread in Jesus's name. Many scholars today believe that their formulation into liturgical rite did not occur until the third century. By the third century, the words and the action of breaking the bread are joined in order to regularize experience. I am always on the look-out for digested histories on topics such as this. I find two to be very helpful. The first is the work of my friend Richard Fabian. Specifically in Fabian's work entitled *Worship at St Gregory's* (San Francisco, CA: All Saints' Company, 1995). The second is Dr. Ros Clarke's work, which is focused upon the literary history of the words of institution and does an excellent job articulating a brief survey of scholarship here: "The Function of the Words of Institution in the Celebration of the Lord's Supper." *The Theologian—The Internet Journal for Integrated Theology*, 2005, accessed July 31, 2017, http://www.theologian.org .uk/church/wordsofinstitution.html.

13. Dom Gregory Dix in *The Shape of Liturgy* (London, UK: Westminister Dacre Press, 1954), C. Kucharek in *The Byzantine-Slav Liturgy of St. John Chrysostom* (Allendale, NJ: Alleluia Press, 1971) and Lionel Mitchell in *The Meaning of Ritual* (Wilton, CT: Morehouse-Barlow, 1988) all connect the *chabûrah* customs with the early Christian liturgy described in both the documents of the *Teaching of the Twelve Apostles* and *The Didache*. I learned this first from Rick Fabian and a longer explanation may be found in *Worship at St. Gregory's*. Fabian, *Worship at St. Gregory's*, 39.

14. Acts 9; see also Galatians.

15. Luke 10:30.

16. Luke 10:31–32.

17. Acts 9:10.

18. Acts 9:11–15.

19. Acts 9:16.

20. Luke 10:33.

21. Acts 9:17.

22. Luke 10:34–36.

23. Acts 9:19–20.

24. Galatians 3:8.

25. See the following for an understanding of how the cognitive maps of the ancient world were broken open by the Christian movement: Gruca-Macaulay, *Lydia*, 233.

25. David Cayley, ed., *The Rivers North of the Future: The Testament of Ivan Illich* (New York: House of Anansi Press, 2011), 31–32.

27. See for further reading Leslie J. Hoppe, *The Synagogues and Churches of Ancient Palestine* (Collegeville, MN: Liturgical Press, 1994).

28. See for further reading Wayne Meeks, *First Urban Christians* (New Haven, CT: Yale University Press, 1983), 80.

29. Ibid., 76–83.

30. For a video presentation of the first Christian communities, an accessible series is produced by PBS and entitled "The First Christians." It aired in 1988 and follows what has remained the basic scholarly understanding of the types of this emerging movement. See L. Michael White and Wayne A. Meeks, "The First Christians: Paul's Congregations," PBS, April 1998, http://www .pbs.org/wgbh/pages/frontline/shows/religion/first/congregations.html.

31. Hauerwas, *Peaceable*, 88.

32. Theologian Stanley Hauerwas clearly defines in his *Peaceable Kingdom* the core of this communal belonging. I am tracing it here as we bring the age of apostolic mission to a close. Hauerwas, *Peaceable*, 87–88.

33. Ibid., 54.

Chapter Five

1. Phyllis Tickle, "Phyllis Tickle: Like an Anthill," Faith and Leadership, August 30, 2010, https://www.faithandleadership.com/multimedia/phyllis -tickle-anthill.

2. Raymond Edward Brown, *The Churches the Apostles Left Behind* (New York: Paulist Press, 1994), 9–19.

3. Kenneth Hylson-Smith, *The Laity in Christian History and Today* (London: SPCK, 2008), 9.

4. Similar hymns include Colossians 1:15–20; 1 Timothy 3:16; Hebrews 1:1–3; and 1 Peter 2:21–25.

5. J. Lebreton and J. Zeilier, *A History of the Primitive Church*, vol. 4 (New York: Collier Books, 1948), 971.

6. For more discussion on this see Meeks, *Urban*, 10–16.

7. Smith, *Laity*, 14–15.

8. Martin Goodman, "Judaism, the Roman Empire and Jesus," in *A World History of Christianity*, ed. Adrian Hastings (Grand Rapids, MI: W.B. Eerdmans, 2000), 22.

9. Marta Sordi and Annabel Bedini, *The Christians and the Roman Empire* (Norman: University of Oklahoma Press, 1994), 189.

10. Edmund H. Oliver, *The Social Achievements of the Christian Church* (Toronto: Ryerson Press, 1930), 30.

11. Tertullian, Apologeticus 39. As quoted in Oliver, *Social*, 29.

12. Paul's letters allude to the fact that some apostles were supported by Christian communities, and it is noteworthy that Paul chose to not make use of this right (see 1 Cor. 9:15). However, the assumption that all early Christian leaders were financially supported in the same way and to the same extent as paid clergy in the modern era is unfounded.

13. Clement, 2 Clementine 16.4. As quoted in Oliver, *Social*, 31. See also *The Didache* on almsgiving.

14. Justo L. González, *The History of Theological Education* (Nashville, TN: Abingdon, 2015), 1–7.

15. Ibid., 9–10.

16. Ibid., 12–13.

17. Meeks, *Urban*, 75.

18. Jonathan Draper, *Gospel Perspectives*, vol. 5, 269, cited in *Didache*, Early Christian Writings, July 20, 2017, http://www.earlychristianwritings.com /didache.html.

19. Cyril C. Richardson, "Didache," in *Early Christian Fathers* (New York: Touchstone, 1996), 128.

20. Ibid.

21. González, *Theological*, 14.

22. Harold H. Rowdon, "Theological Education: A Historical Perspective," *Vox Evangelica* 7 (1971): 75–87.

23. Rowdon, "Theological."

24. Neil Alexander, "The Ordinal" (class discussion, The Episcopal Church College for Bishops, New Bern, NC, June 15, 2018). Bishop Alexander points

out that after a thousand years of Christian ministry priests had become presidents at the table while bishops had become priests who did other things.

25. Alistair C. Stewart, *The Original Bishops: Office and Order in the First Christian Communities* (Grand Rapids, MI: Baker Academic, 2014), 229, 287–98.

26. Stewart, *Original*, 56–101.

27. Alexander, "Ordinal."

28. Edward Foley, *From Age to Age: How Christians Have Celebrated the Eucharist* (Collegeville, MN: Liturgical Press, 2008) 39, 67.

29. Rowdon, "Theological." To read a good synopsis of the theological debates, I suggest Donald K. MacKim, *Theological Turning Points: Major Issues in Christian Thought* (Atlanta: John Knox Press, 1988).

30. Smith, *Laity*, 19–20.

31. Henry Chadwick, *The Early Church* (London: Penguin, 1993), 56–59.

32. Alexander Roberts and James Donaldson, "Constitutions," in *The Ante-Nicene Fathers* (Edinburgh: T. & T. Clark, 1967), 7:389.

33. Roberts and Donaldson, "Constitutions," 475–76.

34. Thomas Macy Finn, *Early Christian Baptism and the Catechumenate* (Collegeville, MN: Liturgical Press, 1992), 43–47.

35. "The Apostolic Canons (xiv, xv), and the Council of Nicæa in 325 (can. xvi) applied this latter term to the territory subject to a bishop. This term was retained in the East, where the Council of Constantinople (381) reserved the word *diocese* for the territory subject to a patriarch (can. ii). In the West also *parochia* was long used to designate an episcopal see. About 850 Leo IV, and about 1095 Urban II, still employed *parochia* to denote the territory subject to the jurisdiction of a bishop. Alexander III (1159-1181) designated under the name of *parochiani* the subjects of a bishop (c. 4, C. X, qu. 1; c. 10, C. IX, qu. 2; c. 9, X, De testibus, II, 20)." Charles George Herbermann, Edward Aloysius Pace, Condé Bénoist Pallen, Thomas Joseph Shahan, John Joseph Wynne, Andrew Alphonsus MacErlean, eds., *The Catholic Encyclopedia: An International Work of Reference on the Constitution, Doctrine, Discipline, and History of the Catholic Church*, Volume 5 (New York, NY: Robert Appleton Company, 1909) I.

Chapter Six

1. Elbert Hubbard, "Hypatia," The Literature Network: Online Classic Literature, Poems, and Quotes. Essays & Summaries, accessed August 2, 2017, http://www.online-literature.com/elbert-hubbard/journeys-vol-ten/10/. Originally published in *Hubbard's Little Journeys Vol. 10: Great Teachers; Hypatia*.

2. Ibid.

3. Luke 22:24; Mark 9:33–37; John 13:27.

4. Rowdon, "Theological."

5. Rowdon, "Theological."
6. Oliver, *Social,* 75.
7. Chadwick, *Early Church,* 58.
8. We see this begin as early as Origen, who while on the one hand rejects violence and idolatry of the Roman army on the other can see that *Pax Romana* and *Pax Christi* are in sync. He writes:

> For righteousness has arisen in His days, and there is abundance of peace, which took its commencement at His birth, God preparing the nations for His teaching, that they might be under one prince, the king of the Romans, and that it might not, owing to the want of union among the nations, caused by the existence of many kingdoms, be more difficult for the apostles of Jesus to accomplish the task enjoined upon them by their Master, when He said, "*Go and teach all nations.*" Moreover it is certain that Jesus was born in the reign of Augustus, who, so to speak, fused together into one monarchy the many populations of the earth. Now the existence of many kingdoms would have been a hindrance to the spread of the doctrine of Jesus throughout the entire world; not only for the reasons mentioned, but also on account of the necessity of men everywhere engaging in war, and fighting on behalf of their native country, which was the case before the times of Augustus, and in periods still more remote. . . . How, then, was it possible for the Gospel doctrine of peace, which does not permit men to take vengeance even upon enemies, to prevail throughout the world, unless at the advent of Jesus a milder spirit had been everywhere introduced into the conduct of things?

> Alexander Roberts, James Donaldson, A. Cleveland Coxe, Allan Menzies, Ernest Cushing Richardson, and Bernhard Pick, "Origen. *Against Celsus,*" in *The Ante-Nicene Fathers: Translations of the Writings of the Fathers down to A.D. 325* (Buffalo: Christian Literature Publishing Company, 1885), vol. 30, book 2, ch. 30.

9. Augustine developed the idea upon Platonist principles while refuting the Donatists. It would again be used during the reformation. It is a theory that simply posits that the visible church is imperfect and filled with sin and brokenness like other institutions. Both Karl Barth and William Stringfellow flat out reject this notion of visible and invisibility. They see that the church must be visible or it is no church at all. And that when the church seeks its worldly preservation or undertakes worldly domination it is no longer the church of Christ—it is an imposter or idolized church. Karl Barth, *Dogmatics in Outline* (New York: Harper & Row, 1959), 142. See also, William Stringfelllow,

Imposters of God: Inquiries into Favorite Idols (Eugene, OR: Wifpf & Stock, 2006), 58.

10. González, *Theological*, 27.
11. Foley, *Age*, 91.
12. Ibid., 113.
13. Ibid., 96–97.
14. González, *Theology*, 35.
15. Alexander, "Ordinal."
16. Ibid. See also J. Neil Alexander, "A Call to Adventure: Seven Propositions on Ministry," in Donald S. Armentrout, *This Sacred History: Anglican Reflections for John Booty* (Cambridge, MA: Cowley Publications, 1990), 29.
17. Ibid.
18. Ibid.
19. Oliver, *Social*, 87.
20. Rowdon, "Theological."
21. González, *Theology*, 41.
22. Cayley, *Rivers*, 87. For a brief history of marriage you might refer to my book *Unity in Mission*.
23. Cayley, *Rivers*, 89. What is also interesting is perhaps that this is the first time women are recognized by the church in any official capacity as individuals with the power and authority to enter into a contract.
24. Ibid., 92–94.

Chapter Seven

1. This quote attributed to Chesterton appears in Nick Page's *A Nearly Infallible History of the Reformation: Commemorating 500 Years of Popes, Protestants, Reformers, Radicals and Other Assorted Irritants* (London: Hodder & Stoughton, 2017).
2. Foley, *Age*, 87.
3. Gerald Strauss, *Manifestations of Discontent in Germany on the Eve of the Reformation: A Collection of Documents* (Bloomington: Indiana University Press, 1985), 40.
4. For further reading on how the age of print affected the Reformation and unified lay movements, see Tessa Watt's *Cheap Print and Popular Piety: 1550–1640* (Cambridge: Cambridge University Press, 1994).
5. Martin Luther, "To the Christian nobility of the German nation concerning the reform of the Christian estate," in *Luther's Works*, eds. Jaroslav Pelikan, Hilton C. Oswald, and Helmut T. Lehmann (St. Louis, MO: Concordia Publishing House, 1986), 44:127, 129.

6. Charles Taylor in his book *A Secular Age* suggests that reason and rational explanations were used by Reformers to remove white magic from the church. These arguments were wielded against the Roman Catholic Church in particular and created a distaste for the old time religion of the age. He wrote: Deism was a response to the "deep-seated moral distaste for the old religion that sees God as an agent in history" [Taylor, *Secular Age*, 274.] Taylor makes the case that it was human freedom that was at the core—the seed of secular humanism. The pure nature of humanity is rooted in its free thinking and action—its nature as a rational agent (p. 282). Taylor goes on to offer that an "interventionist God" is flatly rejected because such a God impedes on human freedom (p. 283). Such a God and such followers of this God must be diminished. Millions were killed in the Thirty Years' War; Cromwell's genocide in Ireland supposedly decreased the population by 40 percent. A quick review of estimates easily convicts us that the *Pax Christiana* of the Reformers was no peace at all.

7. Again, Charles Taylor:

> Around 1500, this drive begins . . . to take up a more ambitious goal, to change the habits and life—practices, not only religious but civil, of whole populations; to instil orderly, sober, disciplined, productive ways of living in everyone. This is the point where the religious drive to reform begins to become interwoven into the attempts to introduce civility, thus to "civilize," as the key term came to be. This was not a simple take-over, a deviation imposed on the drive to religious reform; because religious reformers themselves concurred that the undeniable fruit of Godliness would be ordered, disciplined lives. They also sought to civilize, for good theological reasons. (Taylor, *Secular Age*, 244)

8. Taylor writes that the Reformers suggested the "disenchantment" of religion and the world. All magic, even the "white magic" of the church, had to be purged. This meant that sacraments, religious relics, sacramental prayers were all part of an enchanted world that no longer existed. Therefore, such relics no longer had a place in the work of religion and had to be exorcised. Taylor, *Secular Age*, 72.

9. Professor Kevin Hector offers this perspective of Taylor's work around society, vocation, and the assumptions at the time of the Reformation. Hector writes that Taylor "characterizes 'Reform' as a 'drive to make over the whole society to higher standards,' a drive that is rooted in 'a profound dissatisfaction with the hierarchical equilibrium between lay life and the renunciative vocations' (Taylor, *Secular Age*, 61–63). Advocates of reform were concerned, then, with the fact that the higher life called for by the gospel had come to be seen as a special vocation to be practiced by the elite, rather than as a vocation

to be lived by all Christians. Reform aimed to combat this sort of two-tiered Christianity by insisting that the so called higher life is demanded of every Christian and by putting into effect all sorts of disciplinary measures by means of which to ensure that Christians would live up to this life's demands (Taylor, *Secular Age*, 51). On Taylor's account, then, reform played a key role in producing the sort of 'disciplinary society' that contributed to the eventual development of 'exclusive humanism.' It is important to note, though, that reform may have moved in a different direction if not for the assumption that members of an entire society could be counted as Christian. If one assumes that the church is coterminous with society, it might make sense to try to hold an entire society to higher standards. This assumption is by no means self evident, however. The so called Radical Reformers, for instance, saw this assumption as, in fact, one of the key obstacles to reform and therefore insisted that one counts as a Christian only if one is committed to living the higher life, to submitting oneself to church discipline, and so forth. The point is simply that this assumption seems to play a nontrivial role in the move from reform to the institution of a disciplinary society, for without it, reform might just as well have led to a narrower view of who counts as a member of the church." William Schweiker et al, "Grappling with Charles Taylor's *A Secular Age*," *The Journal of Religion* 90, no. 3 (2010): 367–400.

10. Sometime in December 1522, Luther published "Von Weltlicher Obrigkeit, wie weit man ihr gehorsam schuldig sei," a pamphlet about the relationship of secular powers with God and the Reformation movement. It essentially is a defense of the church's support of the state and its princes. It places the creation of secular powers squarely as one of God's creations for the doing of God's will. Yes, there are limits, but he suggests these in the text. Nevertheless, this reveals how important it was for the Reformers to have the support of the princes for the exercise of reform. See "Martin Luther and the German Princes," Medieval Histories, June 16, 2015, http://www.medievalhistories. com/martin-luther-and-the-german-princes/.

11. We see this similar reformed theology at work in the support of Evangelicals for President Donald Trump, despite the disconnect with other evangelical values.

12. We turn again to Taylor's "anthropocentric turn." Growing out of the Reformation is a continued strengthening of anthropocentrism. God in Christ Jesus becomes a moral guide in the face of modern moral malaise. There was within the church a continued focus upon God as the director of all human agency. Meanwhile, humanism begins to move ever more toward secularism (Taylor, *Secular Age*, 225). The focus was almost all moral conduct (and still is today). The social order was inconvenienced by these virtues and conflicted by them. It is here, then, that philosophers begin to suggest rational atheism over antirational religion (Taylor, *Secular Age*, 266).

13. Smith, *Laity*, 89–90.
14. Bill Bryson, *At Home: An Informal History of Private Life* (London: Doubleday, 2010), 322, 475ff.
15. Robert W. Prichard, *A History of the Episcopal Church* (New York: Morehouse Publishing, 2014), 313.

Chapter Eight

1. Barbara Brown Taylor and Bob Abernathy. "March 9, 2007—Barbara Brown Taylor," Public Broadcasting Service, <http://www.pbs.org/wnet/religionandethics/2007/03/09/march-9-2007-barbara-brown-taylor/1792/>.
2. We do know that comparisons between the different denominations is not a comparison of apples to apples. For instance, the Roman Catholics count numbers who attend Mass at their schools. We do not. Every year The Living Church does a piece on how TEC is losing numbers. It does not do an equally informative piece on the Anglican movement in the Americas, which is interesting and worth noting. You can read their most recent article here: http://livingchurch.org/2017/08/02/episode-1-church-decline/. You can study the numbers for yourself at The Episcopal Church website here: http://www.episcopalchurch.org/library/document/episcopal-congregations-overview-charts; and here: http://www.episcopalchurch.org/files/episcopal_congregations_overview_2014.pdf.
3. David Goodhew's *Growth and Decline in the Anglican Communion: 1980 to the Present* (London: Taylor and Francis, 2016). This is part of the Routledge Contemporary Ecclesiology series.
4. Nathan M. Pusey and Charles L. Taylor, *The Ministry for Tomorrow: Report of the Special Committee on Theological Education* (New York: Seabury Press, 1967), 3–5.
5. Ibid., 9
6. Ibid., 15–21.
7. Ibid., 21.
8. Ibid., 47.
9. Ibid., 46–50.
10. Ibid., 111.
11. This report, every report, and most clergy today do not do the simple economic graphs that show the challenge their individual congregations face when it comes to managing the increasing cost of electricity, heating and cooling the building, and long-term maintenance of aging structures.
12. Donald A. Nickerson et al, "Board of Theological Education," *Report to the 72nd General Convention: Otherwise Known as the Blue Book; Reports and*

Resolutions of the Committees, Commissions, Boards and Agencies of the General Convention of the Protestant Episcopal Church in the United States of America, USA for Consideration in Philadelphia, Pennsylvania, July Sixteenth to Twenty-fifth Inclusive in the Year of Our Lord 1997 (New York: General Convention, 1997), 501–4.

13. Nickerson, "Theological Education," 505.

14. Ibid.

15. Ibid.

16. Ibid.

17. *Reports to the 78th General Convention, Otherwise Known as the Blue Book: Supplementary Materials: Reports of the Committees, Commissions, Agencies and Boards to the General Convention of the Episcopal Church, Salt Lake City, Utah, in the State and Diocese of Utah, June 25–July 3, 2015* (New York: Church Publishing, 2015). 475.

18. Ibid., 476.

19. Ibid.

20. Michael Curry, "The Jesus Movement," Episcopal Church, March 1, 2016. https://www.episcopalchurch.org/posts/publicaffairs/presiding-bishop -michael-curry-jesus-movement-and-we-are-episcopal-church.

21. Daniel Kahneman, *Thinking, Fast and Slow* (New York: Farrar, Straus and Giroux, 2015), 277.

Chapter Nine

1. Ellen Davis, "Growing Into God's Image," The Work of the People, accessed August 10, 2017, http://www.theworkofthepeople.com/growing -into-gods-image

2. Stringfellow, *Imposters*, 51.

3. William Stringfellow reverses the Reformation focus on morality to central-ize the struggle between those who invest in violence and death and those who invest in resurrection. He writes, "It is a distinctive mark of the biblical mind to discern that human history is a drama of death and resurrection and not, as religionists of all sorts suppose, a simplistic conflict of evil vs. good in an abstract sense." Stringfellow, *Imposters*, 64.

4. Ibid., 51.

5. Ibid.

6. Romans 8:35–39.

7. The Book of Common Prayer (New York: Church Publishing, 1979), 381.

8. Humanism became the viable option in the wake of the Reformation and by the nineteenth century was really the only option. The Western mind found a

return to medieval Christianity a lark. Christendom was over. Science and its reformers (Darwin, Freud, Marx) continued to press the argument that religion at its core was nonrational, and even part of the problem. Religion was oppressive and antihuman flourishing. Charles Taylor sees these evolutions of science reach a high point in the 1960s when religion and belief tank in the West. A kind of practical atheism becomes the norm. Taylor, *Secular Age*, 425.

9. Revelation 5:9–10.

10. When John the Baptizer was confronted by soldiers and asked what repentance looked like, John responded, "Don't extort money and don't accuse people falsely—be content with your pay" (Luke 3:14). In other words, John did not force them to give up their profession, but rather asked that they grapple with how their profession as a soldier was at odds with God's inbreaking reign of shalom. I believe that this is work that today's church has neglected in recent years and that this is work that we must courageously lean into if we want to take our vocation as Christians seriously in a secular, violent world.

11. The main reason is idolatry. Early Christians understood that if you served in politics or the army, you had to worship Caesar. The early Christian theologian Tertullian wrote a treatise forbidding military service for Christians. It is entitled *The Crown*. He addresses it again in his treatise entitled *On Idolatry*. Another early Christian theologian Origen condemned military service in his *Divine Institutes*, 6.20. Here he quotes another theologian Lactantius who said, "A just man may not be a soldier." Some vocations in the world require idol worship of weapons, death, and power. Again, Lactantius writes, "Killing itself is banned" and "killing a human being is always wrong." Tertullian wrote, "The Lord, by taking away Peter's sword"—referring to the incident in Gethsemane—"disarmed every soldier thereafter." And he wrote: "We are not allowed to wear any uniform that symbolizes a sinful act." *The Crown* 1.1–6; 11.1–7; 12.1–5; 15.1–4.

12. John Paul II, "*Centesimus Annus*," The Vatican, May 1, 1991, http://w2.vatican .va/content/john-paul-ii/en/encyclicals/documents/hf_jp-ii_enc_01051991 _centesimus-annus.html.

13. Ibid.

14. Wendell Berry, *What Matters? Economics for a Renewed Commonwealth* (Berkeley, CA: Counterpoint, 2010), 8.

15. Herman Daly, "Introduction," in Berry, *What*, 7–8.

16. Ibid.

17. The term *chrematistiscs* is an Aristotelian term that was part of classic economic theory but now has fallen out of disuse. Daly, "Introduction," 7.

18. Berry, *What*, 15.

19. Ibid., 121.

20. Ibid., 51–52.
21. Ibid., 131.
22. Ibid., 94.
23. See Darren Walker's, president of the Ford Foundation, letter regarding the initiative here: https://www.fordfoundation.org/ideas/equals-change-blog /posts/unleashing-the-power-of-endowments-the-next-great-challenge-for -philanthropy.

Chapter Ten

1. Ivan Illich, "Silence Is a Commons" (Address at the "Asahi Symposium Science and Man—The Computer-Managed Society," Tokyo, Japan, March 21, 1982); as published in *The CoEvolution Quarterly* (Winter 1983).
2. Berry, *What*, 51–53.
3. For more information, see my 2016 book entitled *Small Batch*.
4. Rowan Williams, "Human Well-Being and Economic Decision-Making," The Archbishop of Canterbury, November 16, 2009, http://rowanwilliams .archbishopofcanterbury.org/articles.php/767/human-well-being-and -economic-decision-making
5. Ibid.
6. Ibid.
7. Peter Block, Walter Brueggemann, and John McKnight, *An Other Kingdom: Departing the Consumer Culture* (Hoboken, NJ: Wiley, 2016), 37, 64–66.
8. Williams, "Human."
9. Bernd Wannenwetsch, *Political Worship*, trans. Margaret Kohl, Oxford Studies in Theological Ethics (New York: Oxford University Press, 2009), 127.
10. Jean Bethke Elstain, "Christianity and Patriarchy: The Odd Alliance," *Modern Theology*, April 1993, http://onlinelibrary.wiley.com/doi/10.1111/j.1468 -0025.1993.tb00297.x/abstract
11. Wannenwetsch, *Political*, 132–33.
12. Matthew 14:33; 28:9; Luke 24:52; John 9:38.
13. Walter Brueggemann, *Sabbath as Resistance: Saying No to the Culture of Now* (Louisville, KY: Westminster John Knox Press, 2017), 89.
14. Block et al., *Kingdom*, 132.
15. Wendell Berry, "The Loss of the Future," *Manasjournal* 21, no. 47 (November 20, 1968): http://www.manasjournal.org/pdf_library/VolumeXXI_1968 /XXI-47.pdf.
16. Illich, "Silence."
17. Ibid.
18. Ibid.
19. Ibid.

Chapter Eleven

1. Rachel Held Evans, *Searching for Sunday: Loving, Leaving, and Finding the Church* (Nashville, TN: Nelson Books, 2015), 225.
2. Wendell Berry, *The Unsettling of America: Culture & Agriculture* (San Francisco: Sierra Club Books, 1977),19.
3. Ibid., 52.
4. Ivan Illich, Irving Zola, John McKnight, Jonathan Caplan, and Harlan Shaiken, *Disabling Professions* (London: M. Boyars, 2011), 28.
5. Ibid., 19.
6. Ibid., 17–18.
7. Ibid., 78–79.
8. Ibid., 79–80.
9. Ibid., 80–81.
10. Ibid., 82.
11. Stringfellow, *Keeper*, 240–41.
12. Bonhoeffer, *Cost*, 118.
13. Stringfellow, *Keeper*, 241.
14. Stringfellow writes in *Keeper* (241), "The seminary must be reclaimed by the church of Christ."
15. Ivan Illich, *Deschooling Society* (London: Calder & Boyars, 1971), 1.
16. Ibid., 105.
17. Gonzáles, *Theological*, 138.
18. Bonhoeffer, *Cost*, 118.
19. Gonzáles, *Theological*, 138.
20. Ibid.
21. Ibid., 139.
22. Illich, *Deschooling*, 115.
23. Ibid.

Chapter Twelve

1. Pope Francis, "Missa Pro Ecclesia" with the Cardinal Electors, Homily of the Holy Father Pope Francis, Vatican, March 14, 2013, http://w2.vatican.va /content/francesco/en/homilies/2013/documents/papa-francesco_20130314 _omelia-cardinali.html.
2. "My Not Wearing a Mitre," Duncan M. Gray Jr. to Anonymous, September 11, 1986, Episcopal Diocese of Texas: Bishop Diocesan's 2016 Correspondence, Houston, TX.
3. Alexander, "Ordinal." "The ordinal of the 1979 Prayer Book represents a significant shift in our thinking about ordination and roots holy orders more

clearly in a broadly conceived baptismal ecclesiology. Prior to 1979, the American Ordinal reflected the practice of earlier prayer books and focused on an ordination formula that suggested that the bishops imparted some portion of their own power to the person being ordained," says Bishop Alexander.

4. Ibid.
5. Gray Jr., "My Not Wearing a Mitre."
6. BCP, 531. Adapted.
7. A *cathedra* is the bishop's chair in the cathedral.
8. Please see my work on scaleability in the section on diocese in my book *CHURCH* for how this applies to diocesan ministry.
9. Ibid.

Chapter Thirteen

1. Richard Rohr, *The Naked Now: Learning to See as the Mystics See* (New York: Crossroad Publishing, 2015), 23.
2. Exodus 32:1–14.
3. It is possible that the story of the golden calf actually is a reference to a dispute between the later northern and southern kingdoms. See 1 Kings 12:28–30. More than revealing that Israel has one God, the story might reveal that Israel has one place of worship and one kingdom vs a divided one. The theology here is good even if it is a historic controversy in narrative form. Josh Gerstein, "Revisiting the Sin of the Golden Calf," Algemeiner.com, March 16, 2017, https://www.algemeiner.com/2017/03/16/revisiting-the-sin-of-the-golden -calf/. See also Joseph B. Soltoveitchik's *Vision and Leadership* (Brooklyn, NY: KTAV Publishing House, 2012), 131.
4. Jonathan Sacks, *Radical Then, Radical Now* (New York: Continuum, 2004), 129.
5. Rohr, *Naked*, 23.
6. Alexander Roberts, James Donaldson, and A. Cleveland Coxe, eds., "Epistle of Clement to James," in *The Ante-Nicene Fathers, Vol. 8: The Twelve Patriarchs, Excerpts and Epistles, the Clementina, Apocrypha, Decretals, Memoirs of Edessa and Syriac Documents, Remains of the First Ages* (Grand Rapids, MI: Eerdmans, 1978), 220–21.

Bibliography

Alexander, Neil. "The Bishop and the Liturgy." Lecture, Living Our Vows: Episcopal Church Bishop Residency, Roslyn Conference Center, Richmond, Virginia, June 15, 2017.

Bailie, Gil. *Violence Unveiled: Humanity at the Crossroads*. New York: Crossroad, 2004.

Barth, Karl. *Dogmatics in Outline*. New York: Harper & Row, 1959.

Beck, Robert R. *Nonviolent Story: Narrative Conflict Resolution in the Gospel of Mark*. Eugene, OR: Wipf & Stock, 2008.

Bellah, Robert. "Religious Evolution." *American Sociological Review* 29 (1964): 358–74. http://www.jstor.org/stable/2091480?origin=JSTOR-pdf&seq=1#page_scan_tab_contents.

Berry, Wendell. "The Loss of the Future." *Manasjournal* 21, no. 47 (November 20, 1968): http://www.manasjournal.org/pdf_library/VolumeXXI_1968/XXI-47.pdf.

———. *The Unsettling of America: Culture & Agriculture*. San Francisco: Sierra Club Books, 1977.

———. *What Matters?: Economics for a Renewed Commonwealth*. Berkeley, CA: Counterpoint, 2010.

Birkinshaw, Julian. "Managing Complexity Is the Epic Battle Between Emergence and Entropy." *Harvard Business Review*. August 7, 2014. https://hbr.org/2013/11/managing-complexity-is-the-epic-battle-between-emergence-and-entropy.

Block, Peter, Walter Brueggemann, and John McKnight. *An Other Kingdom: Departing the Consumer Culture*. Hoboken, NJ: Wiley, 2016.

Bolz-Weber, Nadia. *Accidental Saints: Finding God in All the Wrong People*. Danvers, MA: Convergent, 2016.

Bonhoeffer, Dietrich. *The Cost of Discipleship*. Godalming, England: Elam Ministries, 2012.

169

———. *Life Together*. Translated by John W. Doberstein. San Francisco: HarperSanFrancisco, 1954.

———. *The Mystery of the Holy Night*. Edited by Manfred Webber. New York: Crossroad, 1996.

Brown, Raymond Edward. *The Churches the Apostles Left Behind*. New York: Paulist Press, 1994.

Brueggemann, Walter. "Evangelism and Discipleship: The God Who Calls, the God Who Sends." *Word and World* 24, no. 2 (2004): 121–35.

———. *Sabbath as Resistance: Saying No to the Culture of Now*. Louisville, KY: Westminster John Knox Press, 2017.

Bryson, Bill. *At Home: An Informal History of Private Life*. London: Doubleday, 2010.

Campbell, Charles L. *The Word before the Powers: An Ethic of Preaching*. Louisville, KY: Westminster John Knox Press, 2002.

Capon, Robert Farrar. *Kingdom, Grace, Judgment: Paradox, Outrage, and Vindication in the Parables of Jesus*. Grand Rapids, MI.: W.B. Eerdmans, 2002.

Cayley, David, ed. *The Rivers North of the Future: The Testament of Ivan Illich*. New York: House of Anansi Press, 2011.

Chadwick, Henry. *The Early Church*. London: Penguin, 1993.

Clarke, Ros. "The Function of the Words of Institution in the Celebration of the Lord's Supper." *The Theologian—The Internet Journal for Integrated Theology*. 2005. http://www.theologian.org.uk/church/wordsofinstitution.html.

Congressional Budget Office. "Trends in Family Wealth, 1989 to 2013." Congressional Budget Office. August 18, 2016. https://www.cbo.gov/publication/51846.

Conybeare, Fred C. "The Survival of Animal Sacrifices inside the Christian Church." *The American Journal of Theology* 7, no. 1 (1903): 62–90. http://www.jstor.org/stable/3154334.

Curry, Michael. "The Jesus Movement." Episcopal Church. March 1, 2016. https://www.episcopalchurch.org/posts/publicaffairs/presiding-bishop-michael-curry-jesus-movement-and-we-are-episcopal-church.

Davis, Ellen. "Growing Into God's Image." The Work of the People. Accessed August 10, 2017. http://www.theworkofthepeople.com/growing-into-gods-image.

Elstain, Jean Bethke. "Christianity and Patriarchy: The Odd Alliance." Modern Theology. April 1993. http://onlinelibrary.wiley.com/doi/10.1111/j.1468-0025.1993.tb00297.x/abstract.

Episcopal Church, The. "Holy Women, Holy Men." Bishop Marmion Resource Center. Accessed March 24, 2017. http://www.bmrc-online.org/app/ResourceView/5/3233.

Evans, Rachel Held. *Searching for Sunday: Loving, Leaving, and Finding the Church*. Nashville, TN: Nelson Books, 2015.

Fabian, Richard. *Worship at St Gregory's*. San Francisco, CA: All Saints' Company, 1995.

Finn, Thomas Macy. *Early Christian Baptism and the Catechumenate*. Collegeville, MN: Liturgical Press, 1992.

Francis, Pope. "Missa Pro Ecclesia" with the Cardinal Electors. Homily of the Holy Father Pope Francis. Vatican. March 14, 2013. http://w2.vatican.va/content /francesco/en/homilies/2013/documents/papa-francesco_20130314 _omelia-cardinali.html.

Gerstein, Josh. "Revisiting the Sin of the Golden Calf." Algemeiner.com. March 16, 2017. https://www.algemeiner.com/2017/03/16/revisiting-the-sin-of-the -golden-calf/.

Girard, René. *Things Hidden Since the Foundation of the World*. Stanford, CA: Stanford University Press, 1987.

González, Justo L. *The History of Theological Education*. Nashville, TN: Abingdon, 2015.

Goodhew, David. *Growth and Decline in the Anglican Communion: 1980 to the Present*. London: Taylor and Francis, 2016.

Grosvenor, B. *Persecution and Cruelty in the Principles, Practices, and Spirit of the Romish Church*. Church of England Pamphlet Collection. 1622.

Gruca-Macaulay, Alexandra. *Lydia as a Rhetorical Construct in Acts*. Atlanta: SBL Press, 2016.

Hastings, Adrian. *A World History of Christianity*. Grand Rapids, MI: W.B. Eerdmans, 2000.

Hauerwas, Stanley. *A Community of Character: Toward a Constructive Christian Social Ethic*. Notre Dame: University of Notre Dame Press, 2010.

———. *The Peaceable Kingdom: A Primer for Christian Ethics*. Notre Dame: University of Notre Dame Press, 2011.

Hauerwas, Stanley, and Travis Reed. "Old Testament Violence." The Work of the People. 2012. Accessed July 21, 2017. http://www.theworkofthepeople.com /old-testament-vilence.

Hauerwas, Stanley, and Travis Reed. "What Is A Christian?" The Work of the People. 2012. Accessed July 20, 2017. http://www.theworkofthepeople.com /what-is-a-christian.

Hays, Richard B. *Echoes of Scripture in the Gospels. S.1.* Waco: TX: Baylor University Press, 2017.

Hinson, E. Glenn. *The Early Church Fathers*. Nashville, TN: Broadman Press, 1980.

Hoppe, Leslie J. *The Synagogues and Churches of Ancient Palestine*. Collegeville, MN: Liturgical Press, 1994.

Howard-Brook, Wes, and Sharon H. Ringe. *The New Testament: Introducing the Way of Discipleship*. Maryknoll, NY: Orbis Books, 2002.

Hubbard, Elbert. "Hypatia." The Literature Network: Online Classic Literature, Poems, and Quotes. Essays & Summaries. Accessed August 2, 2017. http://www.online-literature.com/elbert-hubbard/journeys-vol-ten/10/.Originally published in Hubbard's *Little Journeys Vol. 10: Great Teachers; Hypatia*

Hylson-Smith, Kenneth. *The Laity in Christian History and Today*. London: SPCK, 2008.

Illich, Ivan. *Deschooling Society*. London: Marion Boyars, 2012.

Illich, Ivan, Irving Zola, John McKnight, Jonathan Caplan, and Harlan Shaiken. *Disabling Professions*. New York: M. Boyars, 2011.

Illich, Ivan. "Silence Is a Commons." Address at the "Asahi Symposium Science and Man—The Computer-Managed Society," Tokyo, Japan, March 21, 1982; as published in *The CoEvolution Quarterly* (Winter 1983).

"Institute for the Future." IFTF: Future Work Skills 2020. Accessed August 21, 2017. http://www.iftf.org/futureworkskills.

Jeffrey, David L. *Dictionary of Biblical Tradition in English Literature*. Grand Rapids, MI: W.B. Eerdmans, 1992.

John Paul II. *"Centesimus Annus."* The Vatican. May 1, 1991. http://w2.vatican.va/content/john-paul-ii/en/encyclicals/documents/hf_jp-ii_enc_01051991_centesimus-annus.html.

Kahneman, Daniel. *Thinking, Fast and Slow*. New York: Farrar, Straus and Giroux, 2015.

Kavanaugh, John F. *Following Christ in a Consumer Society: The Spirituality of Cultural Resistance*. Maryknoll, NY: Orbis Books, 2006.

Lebreton, J., and J. Zeilier. *A History of the Primitive Church*. Vol. 4. New York: Collier Books, 1948.

Lupton, Robert D. *Toxic Charity: How Churches and Charities Hurt Those They Help (and How to Reverse It)*. New York: HarperCollins, 2011.

Luther, Martin. *Luther's Works*. Edited by Jaroslav Pelikan, Hilton C. Oswald, and Helmut T. Lehmann. St. Louis, MO: Concordia Publishing House, 1986.

MacKim, Donald K. *Theological Turning Points: Major Issues in Christian Thought*. Atlanta: John Knox Press, 1988.

"Martin Luther and the German Princes." Medieval Histories. June 16, 2015. http://www.medievalhistories.com/martin-luther-and-the-german-princes/.

Meeks, Wayen. *First Urban Christians*. New Haven, CT: Yale University Press, 1983.

McDonald, Brian. "Violence & the Lamb Slain." *Touchstone Archives: Violence & the Lamb Slain.* December 2003. http://www.touchstonemag.com/archives /article.php?id=16-10-040-i.

McNeill, Emily. "Rabbi Jonathan Sacks Explores Roots of Religious Violence." *Cornell Chronicle.* April 21, 2016. http://news.cornell.edu/stories/2016/04 /rabbi-jonathan-sacks-explores-roots-religious-violence.

Merton, Thomas. *New Seeds of Contemplation.* New York: New Directions, 2007.

"My Not Wearing A Mitre." Duncan M. Gray Jr. to Anonymous. September 11, 1986. Episcopal Diocese of Texas: Bishop Diocesan's 2016 Correspondence, Houston, TX.

Myers, Ched. *Binding the Strong Man: A Political Reading of Mark's Story of Jesus.* Maryknoll, NY: Orbis Books, 2008.

———. "The Call of the Rich Man as a Text of Terror." Radical Discipleship. October 11, 2015. https://radicaldiscipleship.net/2015/10/08/the-call-of-the -rich-man-as-a-text-of-terror/.

———. "Jesus' 'Second Call' to Discipleship." Radical Discipleship. February 26, 2015. https://radicaldiscipleship.net/2015/02/26/jesus-second-call-to -discipleship/.

Nickerson, Donald A., et al. *Report to the 72nd General Convention: Otherwise Known as the Blue Book ; Reports and Resolutions of the Committees, Commissions, Boards and Agencies of the General Convention of the Protestant Episcopal Church in the United States of America, USA for Consideration in Philadelphia, Pennsylvania, July Sixteenth to Twenty-fifth Inclusive in the Year of Our Lord 1997.* New York: Church Publishing, 1997.

Oliver, Edmund H. *The Social Achievements of the Christian Church.* Toronto: Ryerson Press, 1930.

Osborne, Kenan B. *Ministry: Lay Ministry in the Roman Catholic Church, Its History and Theology.* Eugene, OR: Wipf & Stock, 2003.

"The Otherness of the Church." John Howard Yoder Digital Library. 2960. Accessed July 24, 2017. http://replica.palni.edu/cdm/ref/collection/p15705 coll18/id/970.

Page, Nick. *A Nearly Infallible History of the Reformation: Commemorating 500 Years of Popes, Protestants, Reformers, Radicals and Other Assorted Irritants.* London: Hodder & Stoughton, 2017.

Percy, William Alexander. *Enzio's Kingdom, and Other Poems.* New Haven, CT: Yale University Press, 1924.

Plato. *Protagoras.* Perseus Digital Library. Accessed August 19, 2017. http://www .perseus.tufts.edu/hopper/text?doc=Perseus%3Atext%3A1999.01.0178%3 Atext%3DProt.

Porterfield, Jason. "The Subversive Magnificat: What Mary Expected the Messiah to Be Like." Enemy Love. January 19, 2013. http://enemylove.com /subversive-magnificat-mary-expected-messiah-to-be-like/.

Prichard, Robert W. A History of the Episcopal Church. New York: Morehouse Publishing, 2014.

Pusey, Nathan M., and Charles L. Taylor. The Ministry for Tomorrow: Report of the Special Committee on Theological Education. New York: Seabury Press, 1967.

Reed, James E., and Ronnie Prevost. A History of Christian Education. Nashville, TN: Broadman & Holman, 1993.

Reports to the 78th General Convention, Otherwise Known as the Blue Book: Supplementary Materials: Reports of the Committees, Commissions, Agencies and Boards to the General Convention of the Episcopal Church, Salt Lake City, Utah, in the State and Diocese of Utah, June 25–July 3, 2015. New York: Church Publishing, 2015.

Richardson, Cyril Charles. Early Christian Fathers. New York: Simon & Schuster, 1996.

Roberts, Alexander, and James Donaldson. The Ante-Nicene Fathers. Vol. 7. Edinburgh: T. & T. Clark, 1967.

Roberts, Alexander, James Donaldson, and A. Cleveland Coxe, eds. The Ante-Nicene Fathers, Vol. 8: The Twelve Patriarchs, Excerpts and Epistles, the Clementina, Apocrypha, Decretals, Memoirs of Edessa and Syriac Documents, Remains of the First Ages. Grand Rapids, MI: Eerdmans, 1978.

Roberts, Alexander, James Donaldson, A. Cleveland Coxe, Allan Menzies, Ernest Cushing Richardson, and Bernhard Pick. The Ante-Nicene Fathers: Translations of the Writings of the Fathers Down to A.D. 325. Buffalo: Christian Literature Publishing Company, 1885.

Rohr, Richard. The Naked Now: Learning to See as the Mystics See. New York: Crossroad, 2015.

Rohr, Richard, and Travis Reed. "Bearing the Divine through the Ordinary." The Work of the People. 2014. Accessed July 22, 2017. http://www.theworkofthe people.com/bearing-the-divine-through-the-ordinary.

Rowdon, Harold J. "Theological Education: A Historical Perspective." Vox Evangelica. 1971. Accessed August 2, 2017. https://biblicalstudies.org.uk/pdf /vox/vol07/education_rowdon.pdf

Russell, Matt. "About Us." Project Curate. 2014. Accessed September 28, 2017. https://www.projectcurate.org/our-mission.

Rutledge, Fleming. The Crucifixion: Understanding the Death of Jesus Christ. Grand Rapids, MI: William B. Eerdmans, 2017.

Sacks, Jonathan. "Bereishit (5769)—Violence in the Name of G-d." Rabbi Sacks. October 25, 2008. http://rabbisacks.org/covenant-conversation-5769 -bereishit-violence-in-the-name-of-g-d/.

———. "Freewill (Vaera 5775)." Rabbi Sacks. January 12, 2015. http://rabbisacks
.org/freewill-vaera-5775/.

———. Not in God's Name: Confronting Religious Violence. New York: Schocken, 2017.

Sayers, Dorothy. "Why Work." TNL Website. 1942. Accessed July 26, 2017. http://tnl.org/wp-content/uploads/Why-Work-Dorothy-Sayers.pdf.

Scarisbrick, J. J. The Reformation and the English People. Oxford, England: Blackwell, 1998.

Schweiker, William et al. "Grappling with Charles Taylor's A Secular Age." The Journal of Religion 90, no. 3 (2010): 367–400. doi:10.1086/651709.

Sebastian, David. "Trends in Theological Education in North America." Lecture, Church of God Theological Administrators' and Instructors Forum, Fritzlar, Germany, March 15, 2010. http://docplayer.net/3887960-Trends-in -theological-education-in-north-america.html.

Skeat, Walter W. An Etymological Dictionary of the English Language. Oxford: Claredon Press, 1897.

Sordi, Marta, and Annabel Bedini. The Christians and the Roman Empire. Norman: University of Oklahoma Press, 1994.

Starr, Mark, and George Barker. A Worker Looks at History: Being Outlines of Industrial History Specially Written for Labour College-Plebs Classes. London: Plebs League, 1919.

Stenton, Doris Mary. English Society in the Early Middle Ages, 1066–1307. Harmondsworth: Penguin, 1991.

Stewart, Alistair C. The Original Bishops: Office and Order in the First Christian Communities. Grand Rapids, MI: Baker Academic, 2014.

Strauss, Gerald. Manifestations of Discontent in Germany on the Eve of the Reformation: A Collection of Documents. Bloomington: Indiana University Press, 1985.

Stringfellow, William. Dissenter in a Great Society: A Christian View of America in Crisis. Nashville, TN: Abingdon Press, 1966.

———. Imposters of God: Inquiries into Favorite Idols. Eugene, OR: Wipf & Stock, 2006.

———. A Keeper of the Word: Selected Writings. Edited by Bill Wylie Kellerman. Grand Rapids, MI: William B. Eerdmans, 1994.

Taylor, Barbara Brown, and Bob Abernathy. "March 9, 2007—Barbara Brown Taylor." PBS. http://www.pbs.org/wnet/religionandethics/2007/03/09/march -9-2007-barbara-brown-taylor/1792/.

Taylor, Charles. A Secular Age. Cambridge, MA: Belknap Press, 2007.

———. Sources of the Self. Cambridge, MA: Harvard Univeristy Press, 1992.

Tickle, Phyllis. "Phyllis Tickle: Like an Anthill." Faith and Leadership. August 30, 2010. https://www.faithandleadership.com/multimedia/phyllis-tickle-anthill.

Walters, James. "William Stringfellow (LSE 1949–50)—a Christian, Not a Moralist." LSE History: London School of Economics and Political Science. June 2016. http://blogs.lse.ac.uk/lsehistory/2016/02/04/william-stringfellow -lse-1949-50-a-christian-not-a-moralist/.

Wannenwetsch, Bernd. *Political Worship.* Oxford Studies in Theological Ethics. Translated by Margaret Kohl. New York: Oxford University Press, 2009.

Watt, Tessa. *Cheap Print and Popular Piety: 1550–1640.* Cambridge: Cambridge University Press, 1994.

Weber, Max. *The Protestant Ethic and the Spirit of Capitalism.* Translated by Talcott Parsons. Kettering, OH: Angelico Press, 2014.

Wells, Sam. "Nazareth Manifesto." *Vagt Lecture: The Nazareth Manifesto.* April 27, 2008. https://web.duke.edu/kenanethics/NazarethManifesto_SamWells.pdf.

Wheatley, Margaret J. *Finding Our Way: Leadership for an Uncertain Time.* San Francisco, CA: Berrett-Koehler Publishers, 2007.

White, L. Michael, and Wayne A. Meeks. "The First Christians: Paul's Congregations." PBS. April 1998. http://www.pbs.org/wgbh/pages/frontline /shows/religion/first/congregations.html.

Williams, Rowan. "Human Well-Being and Economic Decision-Making." The Archbishop of Canterbury. November 16, 2009. http://rowan williams.archbishopofcanterbury.org/articles.php/767/human-well-being -and-economic-decision-making.

Wingren, Gustaf. *Luther on Vocation.* Translated by C. C. Rasmussen. Eugene, OR: Wipf & Stock Publishers, 2004.

Wink, Walter. *Engaging the Powers: Discernment and Resistance in a World of Domination.* Minneapolis, MN: Fortress Press, 1999.

Wright, N.T. "Jesus' Resurrection and Christian Origins." NTWrightPage. Accessed July 31, 2017. http://ntwrightpage.com/2016/07/12/jesus -resurrection-and-christian-origins/.

About the Author

The Rt. Rev. C. Andrew "Andy" Doyle was seated as the ninth bishop of Texas on June 7, 2009, at Christ Church Cathedral, Houston. Born in 1966 in Carbondale, Illinois, and raised in Houston, Bishop Doyle served five years as canon to the ordinary prior to his election. He holds a BFA from the University of North Texas and served at St. Stephen's Episcopal School, Austin, before receiving an MDiv from Virginia Theological Seminary. He is known today for his work in communications, leadership, vision, mission, and writing.

He is the author of *Unity and Mission* (2011); *Unabashedly Episcopalian* (2012), (available in both English and Spanish); *CHURCH: A Generous Community Amplified for the Future* (2015); *A Generous Community: Being Church in a New Missionary Age* (2015); *Small Batch: Local, Organic, and Sustainable Church* (2016); and *The Jesus Heist: Reclaiming The Gospel from the Church* (2017).

He is sought out to participate in innovative conversations about church mission strategy, structures, and communications in an amplified world filled with digital natives. Today he is interested in how our conversations inside the church may contribute to a paralyzed mission, and the nature of the vocation of the church itself and the church's vocations.

His six-word autobiography is "Met Jesus on Pilgrimage, still walking."

He enjoys classic rock vinyl from the 1960s and 1970s; genealogy; painting; and writing. He is married to JoAnne and they have two children.